KU-358-800

29. vi. 79

GENERAL STAFFS AND DIPLOMACY
BEFORE THE SECOND WORLD WAR

GENERAL STAFFS AND DIPLOMACY BEFORE THE SECOND WORLD WAR

EDITED BY ADRIAN PRESTON

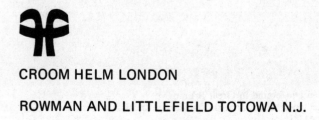

CROOM HELM LONDON

ROWMAN AND LITTLEFIELD TOTOWA N.J.

©1978 Croom Helm
Croom Helm Ltd, 2-10 St John's Road, London SW11

British Library Cataloguing in Publication Data

General staffs and diplomacy before the Second World War.
    1. World war, 1939-1945 – Diplomatic history
    2. Diplomacy – History – 20th century
    3. Armies – Staffs – History – 20th century
    I. Preston, Adrian
    327'.2   D748

ISBN 0-85664-650-4

First published in the United States 1978 by
Rowman and Littlefield
81 Adams Drive
Totowa, New Jersey

ISBN 0-8476-6075-3

Printed and bound in Great Britain
by Redwood Burn Limited, Trowbridge and Esher

CONTENTS

PREFACE AND ACKNOWLEDGEMENTS

The essays comprising this book were originally read to the Fourth Annual Military History Symposium held at the Royal Military College of Canada on 31 March and 1 April 1977. The theme of this Symposium, like that of its predecessors, was not a strictly military one and was consistent with the kind of approach which the Department of History has always taken to the study of warfare and social order. In some measure, this particular theme was inspired by Donald Watt's Lees-Knowles' Lectures, published in 1976 as *Too Serious a Business*, which struck us as being one of the most original and potentially one of the most provocative attempts to re-examine the origins of the Second World War, both in terms of the documents released by the Thirty-Year Rule and in terms of the post-war drift of Anglo-European politics.

The nature of the subject, as we visualised it from behind the stone-built walls of RMC, would call not so much for specialists in the technical development or planning functions of General Staffs as for contemporary historians whose grounding lay primarily in diplomacy and international politics. We hoped that they would examine the great questions of European security and order, both national and collective, as much through the eyes of Cabinets and Foreign Offices as through those of Chiefs of Staff.

Because we accepted, for the purposes of the Symposium, Donald Watt's argument that the first two years of formal warfare (1939-41) — before the entrance of the United States, Japan and Russia — constituted a state of European 'civil war', we did not feel that the inclusion of the Canadian prewar experience was at all appropriate or necessary. Certainly, it would have interjected a bizarre and trifling element into what was otherwise, intellectually and geographically, a reasonably compact and unified theme.

Not all Canadians would have agreed with us. Yet it might have consoled them to know that Canadian scholars such as John Cairns, Sydney Aster, Neville Thompson, Peter Dennis, Lawrence Pratt and Ken Calder (originally working towards British and American doctorates, it might be noted) have done some of the best and freshest work in a field which, despite its closeness to us in time, is already showing signs of becoming dangerously overwritten. Because others bolder and better equipped have written extensively upon the historiography of the

Preface and Acknowledgements

origins of World War II, we felt no editorial compulsion to add to the labours of Sisyphus.

As in the past, it is a pleasure to thank the Department of National Defence and the Canada Council for the assistance, financial and administrative, which made it possible for RMC to enjoy the company of its speakers and guests for several days. Sergeant MacLean and Mr Fawkes of the Senior Staff Mess, Sergeant Tupin and Mrs Hope of the Transportation Section and Mrs Karen Brown of the Department of History were especially helpful in making the Symposium run as smoothly as it did.

Adrian Preston

1 EUROPEAN MILITARY LEADERSHIP AND THE BREAKDOWN OF EUROPE, 1919-1939

D.C. Watt

The purpose of this paper is to resume the argument I advanced in the lectures I gave in Cambridge in 1973, which were republished by Maurice Temple Smith and California as *Too Serious a Business* two years later.[1] In those lectures, I argued that historians writing of the origins of the Second World War and of the first two years of its course had come to concentrate too exclusively on that version of events which depicted it as yet another struggle between independent nation states for mastery and dominion. Many contemporary observers, and many of the participants, I argued, saw the events of the years 1931-41, if not of the whole inter period, as forming not an international war but a civil war covering most of Europe. For historians to ignore or to dismiss these perceptions, formed and expressed as they were by the participants themselves, would be both arrogant and stupid. It would be a betrayal of the historians' professional duty. But a civil war is one *within* a particular *civis*, a particular society. In what sense, then, did the participants and contemporary observers consider 'Europe' to be a society? What did they mean by 'Europe'? Clearly they were not talking in terms of a European state or of European union, even though research is now showing that there was much more support for this idea among conservative elements in Europe at the time M. Briand advanced his famous plan than British historians have so far allowed.

At this point I recalled the passage in J.M. Keynes' brilliant *Economic Consequences of the Peace*[2] in which he reminded his readers how before 1914 in many important economic and social respects there were no national barriers to the flow of money, travel, immigration, investment or information over all but a few of the most backward and tyrannical corners of the globe. It is true that the terms in which he couches this passage makes it clear that he is talking in terms of the reasonably wealthy educated upper and upper middle classes of the day, the aristocracy, the *noblesse de la robe*, the *haute bourgeoisie*, and the most successful of the new professional classes. I have called it a Harrods' eye view of life. That magnificent London store then as now boasts that there is nothing it cannot order the world over given a client sufficient well-heeled. I recalled too that Keynes' career continued until well into the post Second World War era; and that whereas historians have come to view the pre-1914 and the inter-war years as two quite separate periods, they share to a considerable degree the same *dramatis personae*, even though by 1939 the main roles are being played by actors who played only minor roles, some-times only to the extent of being spear carriers, crowd members or noises off, before 1914.

Here it was clear that the major historians had passed through and beyond the stage of regarding Europe simply as a geographical expression covering a number of unrelated nation states, separate in language, culture, race and ethical outlook one from another, engaged in a Darwinian struggle for survival in a Hobbesian world. Few would now describe the state of international relations before 1914, as Lowes Dickinson did, as the international anarchy. Instead one had studies like that of Carsten Holbraad,[3] echoing the much older work of R.B. Mowat on the Concert of Europe.[4] One had Stuart Hughes' brilliant study of the growth of a European consciousness in his *Con-sciousness and Society.*[5] There is Professor Lyons' study of interna-tionalism before 1914, ranging from attempts in Volapük and Esperanto to develop a common language to the growth of the great international professional, educational and scientific associations, not forgetting the Olympic movement itself.[6] There was Herbert Feis' pioneer study of *Europe, the World's Banker.*[7] That so much of this internationalism had failed to survive the bitterness of the First World War did not invalidate it as a field of historical study or diminish its relevance to the questions I was asking.

I remembered too the contrast Professor A.E. Campbell drew twenty years ago between the British reactions to President Cleveland's inter-vention in the Anglo-Venezuelan frontier dispute and to the Kaiser's message to President Kruger after the failure of the Jameson Raid.[8] The first, he wrote, was largely ignored, despite the intemperance of President Cleveland's language, on the grounds that the American did not know what he was doing. The second provoked angry public reaction and the mobilisation of the Flying Squadron. The Kaiser, it was felt, knew only too well what he was doing. The Kaiser was a member of the club. He understood the rules. President Cleveland did not.

How then could the 'club' be described? At this point two sets of concepts presented themselves. The one had to do with systems of states, laws, rules, conventions and power relationships. The other had to do with social relationships which spilt over and across the boun-daries which divide state from state, relationships sufficiently numerous themselves to form a kind of society. It is the essence of such relationships within that kind of society that we call a plural society that the individual belongs to a wide variety of sets of relationships, some formal and institutional, some informal, some prescribed, some optional. Each set gives him a sense of belonging, with each he feels a kind of self identification, to each he feels a sort of loyalty. Once such relationships — some of which are political, some economic, some social in the narrow sense, some cultural — are recognised as spilling across national boundaries, one has what Raymond Aron has described as a trans-national society.[9] And when conflict ensues one has the same process of pull-devil, pull-baker in the field of loyalties and identifications as one has with the disintegration or polarisation of social relationships *within* a single state when civil war breaks out. The degree of hatred is compounded by the feeling of betrayal.

I was left therefore with three sets of propositions. The first had to do with Europe being, before 1914, both a states-system and a trans-national society which was plunged in 1914 into a conflict remarkably like a civil war. The second had to do with Europe between 1919 and 1939, and the degree to which memories of the pre-1914 system and its breakdown conditioned the conduct of state policy within Europe. The third had to do with the role of the military within this process.

But before I could proceed to examine these propositions further, there were three further sets of questions to examine arising from the use of the word Europe. What states were members of the European system? What elements could be described as part of the transnational society? And how could the analysis of a set of formal relationships between states be reconciled with that of a series of clusters of social relationships within a transnational society?

This last set of questions, however, presented no real problem to anyone formally trained as a diplomatic historian. Anyone who sets out to answer the kinds of questions that beset the path of the historian of diplomacy is at once made aware that the figures whose initials and signatures bestrew the telegrams, despatches, minutes and memoranda which make up the raw material of his trade are a small, easily definable and easily identifiable elite group. The processes of policy-making relate them to other equally small and identifiable elite groups, in politics, in the armed services, in the domestic bureaucracy, in commerce, finance and industry and among the leaders and formulators of publicly expressed opinions. To understand these processes one has to be able to chart, as the individual biographer does, the networks of informal relationships as well as the more formal channels of communication between them. But both formal legal relations and informal social contacts and ties are entertained by the same individuals. The distinctions are intellectual, conceptual rather than real. Moreover, if this is true within the frameworks of individual states it does not cease to be valid when the boundaries of these states are transcended.

The states of which lawyers and theorists of international relations speak are only abstractions of intellectual argument abstracted for the purposes of their argument. In reality they are shorthand terms concealing or embodying clusters of small, identifiable, interrelated elites; some of these are more engaged in international and in transnational relationships than others. Beyond them there are the numerically much larger sections of the population who vote, read and write to the newspapers, pay taxes and may ultimately be called upon to fight, even to lay down their lives, for their country. Their prejudices, inhibitions, perceptions, sensitivities and insensitivities set the limits within which the governing elites exercise that governance. They do not have much to do in a direct way with the relationships which make up the transnational element in their society, save at the economic and perhaps at the cultural level. It is on the elite groups that study must mainly be concentrated.[10]

To decide which states are members of the European states system and the European transnational society is more difficult. One is driven to employ a range of criteria rather than a single yardstick. Obviously, one set of criteria has to do with the terms of the formal relationships between states. During the 1920s for example, the Soviet Union found itself the target for British and French intervention, at least in the years 1918-20. It reacted by creating a security system on its frontiers of bilateral non-aggression pacts whose format made it quite clear that they were concluded between members of different, potentially hostile socio-political systems.

The United States failed to ratify the treaty of Versailles. In the Washington Treaties of 1922 and the Kellogg-Briand Pact of 1928, its statesmen were self-confessedly trying to set up a system of international relationships which unlike the League of Nations would acknowledge American initiative and leadership. From 1926 to 1934, the United States approached much closer to Europe, participating in the work of the preparatory commission to the disarmament convention, aiding the pacification of the reparations issue, intervening in the chaos of 1931 with the Hoover Moratorium. But with Roosevelt's advent in 1933, the devaluation of the dollar, the break-up of the London Economic Conference, the neutrality legislation of 1935-6,

America can hardly be described as taking any significant part in the European states system.

The Soviet Union, on the other hand, joined the League in 1934 and in 1935 proclaimed the Popular Front against Fascism. Behind this, however, the Five Year Plan was creating the conditions of economic autarky and the Great Purges were destroying all the informal social ties between the Soviet ruling elites and their European counterparts by destroying very large parts of those elites themselves.[11] The Soviet leadership corps of 1939 bore very little resemblance to that of 1934. The Nazi-Soviet pact of 1939 made formal a relationship with Europe that had never really changed even in the days of the Franco-Soviet pact and the Popular Front.

It is clear therefore that in the years 1933-9 neither the American nor the Soviet leadership, nor, it should be added, any significant part of American opinion, thought of their countries as being in any way involved in the European states system, even when that system was on the point of plunging itself into internecine war for the second time in their lifetimes. This does not imply that they did not entertain the fear that the conflict might get out of hand, nor that they did not have their preferences as to the outcome of the conflict. But the war in Europe was for them essentially a spectator sport.

It is a curious historical paradox that during the interwar period both America and Soviet Russia had become in different ways part of the mental furniture of Europe, not perhaps of the governing elites, but certainly of the internal intellectual elites and of their more general publics. In addition the Soviet leadership had since 1917 been more generally involved in European politics through its links with the European revolutionary working-class movement and its intellectual bourgeois hangers-on.[12] As long as Willi Muenzenberg remained free to organise the International Workers Help movement and to manufacture Fronts for peace and anti-fascism, to which both politically-minded workers and disaffected bourgeois intellectuals could be attracted, the Soviet leadership remained somewhat more than merely a piece of their mental furniture.[13] The progressive Stalinisation of the leadership of the various European Communist party leaderships gradually reduced the substance of this position to a shadow: the conclusion of the Nazi-Soviet pact caused the shadow to disappear almost completely.

The United States by contrast had played an active part in the economic life of Europe up to 1929 or so and an equally active part in its political life until Roosevelt's assumption of office. Thereafter it became a creature existing only in European fantasy. At the elite level

America featured only as the ultimate *dea ex machina* in a new war, one which in the meantime it would be a waste of time to court and folly to antagonise. For a small section of the intellectual bourgeoisie and the political leadership in England continued to entertain the dream of Anglo-American hegemony. A slightly larger section saw in the New Deal a populist democratic solution to the dilemmas of the time.[14]

The main pull of America, however, was felt by the lower middle and working classes of Europe, the land of Hy-Brasil, where all the women were beautiful, even the poor were rich, where there were no caste or class barriers to ambition, where everyone had a bathroom, a car, a vote, and honesty always prevailed over corruption. Hollywood's America became so essential a part of the mental furniture of the British public that even at the height of Germany's submarine offensive, valuable shipping space and even more valuable dollars had to be reserved for the import of American film.

Was Britain part of Europe? The short answer must be that for many of the interwar years most parts of British opinion both at the elite and the mass level would have answered this question with a negative. Opinion seesawed between concern and indifference, jingoistic isolation and concerned participation. Isolationism masqueraded in various guises including even concern for collective security. But the objective realities, trade, finance, vulnerability to air attack, eliminated the extra-European alternatives. From 1933 onwards, even though British military planners were barred from preparing for a major continental war, both political and strategic imperatives drove Britain, as they had driven her over the previous four centuries, into the leadership of a European coalition against Europe's would-be conqueror.[15] Even after Britain's expulsion from the continent she retained the leadership of that coalition from Europe's governments in exile to their conquered subjects huddled in darkness over their radio sets to listen to the last voice of the democratic tradition in Europe, the BBC.

Let me now return to the European military leaderships. It is my contention that the course of events in Europe between 1930 and 1939 marks the second breakdown this century of Europe as a states system[16] and as a transnational society in the sense in which Raymond Aron deployed this concept. This system, this society, was itself the result of an attempt to recreate the transnational society and political states system as it had been experienced in Europe before 1914, an attempt undertaken by a generation educated within, conditioned by and largely anxious to return to that society and system, suitably purged of course of the faults which had led to its breakdown.

Before 1914 that society had existed primarily at the elite level, aristocracy, *haute bourgeoisie*, and among the leadership of the professional classes whose wealth, prestige and influence in the state had begun to emerge in the last decades of the nineteenth century. It existed as a political system, as a set of economic relationships precariously balanced between nationalist competition and supranationalist combination, and as a set of social, societal and cultural relationships. As a political system its functioning was based on the acceptance by the ruling, decision-making elites of common political concerns, hopes of assistance, fears of war. They accepted a set of rules and conventions, whose strength approximated to that of customary law and whose transgression was immediately recognisable. They observed a series of treaties, the collection and publication of which was one of the first tasks of the newly growing scholarly discipline of international relations and their history. They had begun too to evolve institutions of international co-operation at both the political and the economic level, such as regular congresses, standing committees of ambassadors, arbitration commissions, conventions of international jurists, consortia of bankers, international trading companies, international technical conventions on posts and telegraphs. At the social and cultural level the nobility and the *haute bourgeoisie* intermingled socially, took their pleasure and leisure together and more than occasionally intermarried. International scientific, academic, social and sporting associations sprang up including the Olympic movement. They share if not the reality at least the assumption that there was a European culture and heritage from classical Greece onwards of which they were all the inheritors.

The elite groups of this transnational society enjoyed a double set of relationships, to each other within the political, institutional and social framework of their particular nation state, and to each other within the political and economic systems, the rules, conventions and customary laws and the social and cultural relationships which taken together made of Europe a transnational society.

The role of the military leadership groups was anchored firmly to the framework, the structure of the nation state; of all the elite groups in the transnational society they seem in ethos and attitude most schismatic, dedicated to the defence of the nation and nothing beyond this. An essential element in the maintenance of the European political system however was the power relationships between its members both as allies and potential adversaries. The maintenance of these power relationships was the task of the military leaderships of the various

powers. Before 1914, important elements among these military leadership groups began to devote their energies not to maintaining but to dis-
rupting those power relationships.

The military leadership groups also played an important internal role
in maintaining the support on which the traditionalist deferential
societies of the individual nation states rested and without which transnational relationships between the leadership groups of the individual
states could not have been possible. They were tied into and largely
recruited from the landowning nobility. Their position was enhanced by
the universal or near-universal conviction that government divides
itself into the civil and the military spheres, one headed by the chief
political adviser to the head of state, the other by his chief military
adviser. The military leadership, in brief, supported the states system
which made up the political dimension of European society. They were
not, as such, part of the transnational society in its economic, social or
cultural dimensions, save by virtue of their membership of the aristocracy in their own countries. They might intermarry; and where
dynastic connections had grown unusually complex they could, like
Prince Louis of Battenberg, end up in the armed forces of countries
other than those in which they were born.

The events of the decade 1914-24 changed the nature of prewar
European society radically both at the level of individual states and, as
an inevitable consequence, at the transnational level. Three sets of
events are of critical importance: the defeat of the central powers, the
example of revolution in Russia, and the runaway inflation of the years
1919-24. At the national level, the last elements of power of the aristocracy and nobility of central Europe were destroyed. Their losses
among the young of their class were exceedingly heavy both at the
various fronts and from the blockade and the epidemic of Spanish in-
fluenza. They lost their pre-eminence among the officer class with the
massive influx of officers of bourgeois origin necessitated by the
casualty rates of the years 1914-16. The inflation of 1919-24 destroyed
the basis of their wealth in many cases. The disappearance of the
Hapsburg empire, the destruction of the Prussian franchise system, the
revolutions which destroyed the German monarchies and their courts
wrought even more destruction. Only in the officer corps of the
100,000-man German army was a section of the German nobility preserved in power and influence. As an element in a transnational society
they disappeared entirely.

The *haute bourgeoisie* were less immediately affected by the war and
the inflation. True, they lost a great deal of money in the repudiation of

Russia's prewar debts and the collapse of the Austro-Hungarian and Ottoman empires. Where their wealth was based on industry, trade or banking however they were too essential to the new European states for their losses to damage them collectively for long. Their losses were psychological rather than directly political. They were, none the less, deeply traumatic. Before 1914 they had been part of a society which was hierarchically organised, based on deference upward and authority downwards in the system of relationships of which it was comprised. Many had resented their exclusion from the ultimate heights of that hierarchy; but they had been sapping those heights with their wealth, advancing as their English exemplars had by marriage and by other forms of purchase. The war and the revolution had destroyed that system, seemingly irretrievably, and the whole concept of hierarchy and deference with it. The wealthy bourgeoisie of Europe could live with parliamentary democracy; they could not live with confiscation, nationalisation or workers' soviets. From 1919 onwards they were running scared, scared of what they called Bolshevism, and of revolution. In political terms this meant a much greater concern with domestic political and social stability than before.

In international terms the attitudes of the governing elites were changed too by the events of 1914-24. British elite opinion, as already noted, recoiled emotionally from Europe, seeking identification with the emergent Commonwealth, even with the United States. Economic and financial opinion looked to a restoration of the gold standard and of London's financial pre-eminence. German elite opinion became largely obsessed with the destruction of the Treaty of Versailles, French with its maintenance. No one had much confidence in the rules and conventions by which international relations had been governed before 1914. Instead, opinion in Britain and France had tended to look to the substitution of a formal association of nations based on a written constitution into which both the unwritten rules and conventions and the fledgling institutions of pre-1914 Europe could be absorbed. Under American urging, fed on the opinion of British radicals, these trends coalesced in the Covenant of the League of Nations. America's failure to ratify the Treaty of Versailles and the exclusion of the Soviet Union made the League, despite its Asiatic, Latin American and Commonwealth membership, largely European in its orientation and its concerns.

The European system of the interwar years was a frail and sickly concern. It functioned at its best in the years 1924-30. By 1931, the year of the abortive Austro-German customs union and the collapse of the Bank of England, it was already in its death throes; the following year brought with Lausanne and the meeting of the World Disarmament Conference faint hopes of its revival; with Hitler's appointment as Reichschancellor in January 1933 it was foredoomed. While the outbreak of the second European civil war in this century was to be delayed until the end of August 1939, neither its inevitability nor its outcome could be denied for much longer.

What part then did the military play in all this? The short answer is that they played four roles, all essentially negative. The first is that they failed in any way to underwrite the political functioning of the League of Nations and the European political and security system it prescribed. The second is that they failed in important respects to uphold the domestic systems of their countries from which they felt increasingly isolated and with which they felt increasingly unable or unwilling to identify. The third is that they failed to keep abreast of changes in the technology of war and therefore in their comprehension of the realities of power and force in international relations. And fourthly they failed as Cassandras to prevent their political overlords from a new recourse to that force, even where their forebodings were to be more than amply confirmed by the outcome. To say that they failed is not to pin blame or responsibility for these failures exclusively or even partially on them. The military function within a framework of civil-military relationships in which the political rulers have ultimate control and which depends for its proper functioning on both civil and military participants understanding the realities of each other's position.

If one is to evaluate the four areas of military failure it would not be fair to ascribe major responsibility to the military participants in any but the second and third roles, the failure to uphold the domestic political systems of their countries and to keep abreast of changes in the technology of war. But in these the French army's antagonism or indifference towards the political leadership of the Third Republic, and the Reichswehr's encouragement of intrigue at the top and *Nursoldatentum* at all other levels stand pre-eminent. The British armed forces were the most firmly integrated into the governing elites. The leadership of the Italian armed forces displayed a frivolity of purpose for which it is difficult to find historical parallel. The Soviet military leadership was to be largely destroyed by Stalin,[17] for reasons which still for the main part elude our comprehension.

Where the first role, the upholding of the League of Nations and the European security system linked with this is concerned, the military leaderships of the European powers found themselves in a singularly unfortunate position. The German military leadership had no reason whatever to support a system the intention and effect of which was to prevent them from fulfilling their professional responsibilities. Denied tanks, aeroplanes, heavy guns, a fortified western frontier, a modern navy and a mass army their military projections in the 1920s were so uniformly pessimistic it was hardly surprising that they should seek to evade them in every possible way, including the exploitation of relations with the Red Army to the utmost possible degree.

The leadership of the French army was in almost equal difficulty. In 1919 they had looked to the establishment of a separate Rhineland state and the permanent occupation of bridgeheads over the Rhine. Their advice had not been sought on the network of alliances in Eastern Europe into which their political bosses were to enter. Their attempts to prevent separatism in the occupied Rhineland and the use of reparations as a device to keep Germany weak blew up in their hands. The Maginot Line was the logical outcome. That the Quai d'Orsay, the Assemblée Nationale and successive occupants of the Elysée failed to understand its strategic implications for the policy of alliance in Eastern Europe is hardly their fault, since the Maginot Line was constructed with the wholehearted support of all three.

The Chiefs of Staff in Britain were equally disenchanted with the League. Their reasoning was far from the Neanderthal parodies invented by David Low, the cartoonist, to put into the mouth of his eponymous Colonel Blimp. They objected to it because they thought its concept essentially fraudulent. It was dedicated to the ideal of national disarmament to the lowest levels consistent with national security. Yet its provisions for international security required its members to accept an open-ended commitment to commit forces anywhere in the world against any enemy. This they saw as military and strategic nonsense based at best on a bluff. They therefore opposed the Draft Treaty of Mutual Guarantee and the Geneva Protocol, accepted Locarno against their better judgement, and rejected action in support of the League in successive crises, over Corfu in 1924, over Manchuria and over Ethiopia. Their advice was accepted by their political overlords in all these cases; only in the last was any substantial section of British opinion in general disagreement with them.

The clearest case of military responsibility for the final breakdown of Europe's transnational society would seem, at first sight, to lie in their general failure to keep abreast of the changing technology of war. This is, after all, a matter which could well be regarded as supremely one of military responsibility. How could, how can the civilian political leadership of a state, or the opinion of the constituencies from which they draw their power, be expected to arrive at a correct evaluation of the degree to which technological change is altering their general security without guidance from their professional military advisers? In the twentieth century technological advance which had already enormously enhanced the defensive by multiplying the fire power of the individual military unit with the machine gun and barbed wire, added a third dimension, that of the air, to the battlefield and by so doing enormously extended the depth of the area in which the armed forces and the civilian population of a state might expect to be attacked by their enemy. It had then provided armour and cross-country mobility to the offensive with the development of the tank. With motorised transport it had immensely improved the supply position of armies in the field. Poison gas finally seemed to have provided a way of killing with no hazard to the user. At sea, the submarine made the privateer, the operator of the *guerre de course*, invisible and seemed for a time to have made old doctrines of the command of the sea irrelevant.

The Second World War produced four major adaptations of technological advance to the battlefield, each of which gave their pioneer users victory in the field against the apparent balance of forces. These were the combination of divebomber and tank which made the *Blitzkrieg* so irresistible on the battlefield from 1939 to 1943; the combination of radio-location and ground-to-air communication system with the fast single-wing all-metal monoplane which made possible the central direction of air defence and defeated both the German air offensive against Britain in 1940 and that of the Allies against the German cities in 1943; the adaptation of war in the air to the sea which made possible the Japanese and American long-range naval victories of 1942 in the Pacific, and the British or perhaps the Anglo-American defeat of the German submarine in 1943;and lastly the atom bomb.

The first of these destroyed France and the French army in the field and gave the Germans victory over the armies of Britain and the Soviet Union from which only geography rescued them. The second contained and defeated what had seemed to be an irresistible way of waging war at a distance, the strategic bombing offensive. The third destroyed all forms of conventional sea power, making the battleship as obsolete as the galleon or the phalanx. The fourth seemed to have destroyed conventional war as such. The armies of France, Britain and the Soviet Union stand convicted of failure to develop or to anticipate the development of the first technique. The second made nonsense of the dominant doctrines of air warfare developed in the British air ministry, by the

Luftwaffe and the Regia Aeronautica, and, it may be added, by the US
Army Air Force. (Neither the French Armée de l'Air nor the Soviet Air
Force can strictly be said to have evolved any doctrines of war in the
air whatever.) The third defeated the naval theorists of the Royal Navy
and the Reichsmarine.

And yet when one seeks to ascribe responsibility for these failures to
the professional military advisers of the defeated it appears extremely
difficult in many cases to limit it to them and them alone. The British
failures stem from a debate between advocates of the strategic bombing
offensive as the only form air warfare should take which in itself prevented both military and naval war staffs from developing their
thinking to admit the dimension of air warfare to their own areas of
war. In the end this can be traced to the separation of the Royal Air
Force from the Army and the Royal Navy, a decision taken by Britain's
political heads as a result of civilian technological fantasising. And it was
civilian pressure which ensured that the Air Ministry was made to take
part in the air defence of Great Britain in the 1930s, gave them radar,
the Spitfire and the Hurricane and the ground control system which
brought victory in 1940. The French failures stem not only from military
conservatism but from the doctrine of the nation in arms which was essentially a political rather than a military creed opposed to the elitism
preached by de Gaulle. German failures stemmed from the acceptance by
the military of political goals which simply did not necessitate any thought
on the need to wage war further than fifty miles' depth from the current
front line. The Soviet failures seem equally to have stemmed as much from
the politicisation of Soviet military doctrine as from any technical defic-
iences in the development of military thought. The atom bomb is entirely
the product of civilian science and a civilian attitude to war as in itself so
horrible that any means of ending it, no matter how horrible, is to be preferred — a paradox as much of emotion and unreason as of logic.

Finally the armed forces failed as Cassandras. Here their failure
stems from a breakdown in civil-military relationships which was itself
part of the general breakdown of the political systems in their individual
countries and in the European system as such. It must of course be
admitted that in 1938 the Cassandras did not fail to obtain a hearing,
save perhaps in Germany. By 1939, the British Chiefs of Staff had
abandoned the role. The German General Staff, bemused by Hitler's
success in September 1938 and paralysed by their hatred of Poland, had
largely sunk back into *Nursoldatentum*. The Italians prevailed upon
Mussolini to remain neutral. The French remained wrapped in a cloak
of gloom; yet France had no choice but to follow Britain. As for the

Soviets, the attitude of the Soviet military staff remains 'a mystery wrapped in an enigma'. One cannot however resist hazarding a guess that the defensive posture and apparent defeatism projected by the British and French participants in the Moscow staff talks in August 1939 can have done nothing to discourage Soviet military support for the policy of neutrality embodied in the conclusion of the Nazi-Soviet pact.

To sum up: the military advisers of the European powers still seem to bear a very considerable burden of responsibility for the outbreak of the First World War and the destruction it wrought on European society. For the political developments of the interwar period, the breakdown of the structure of traditional civilian politics in Europe between the wars, they must carry their share of responsibility. In the events which led to the outbreak of the Second World War in Europe, the destruction of the European system and the bringing-in of the super powers, their part is not unimportant, but it is negative rather than positive, a failure to restrain rather than an urge towards action. For this, the discredit brought on them by their record in the events of 1914-18 is not the least of the contributing factors. For as E.H. Carr wrote years ago, the events of 1919-1939 constitute only a twenty years' armistice; though today we might well consider them an armistice in a rather different war from that of which he wrote.

Notes

1.   *Too Serious a Business. European Armed Forces and the Approach of the Second World War.* London and Berkeley, California, 1975.
2.   J.M. Keynes, *The Economic Consequences of the Peace,* London, 1920, pp. 9-10.
3.   Carsten Holbraad, *The Concert of Europe: a study in German and British International Theory 1815-1914,* London, 1970.
4.   R.B. Mowat, *The Concert of Europe,* London, 1970.
5.   H. Stuart Hughes, *Consciousness and Society, The Reorientation of European Thought, 1890-1930,* London, 1959.
6.   F.S.L. Lyons, *Internationalism in Europe, 1815-1914,* Leyden, 1963.
7.   Herbert Feis, *Europe, the World's Banker,* New York, 1930.
8.   A.E. Campbell, *Great Britain and the United States, 1895-1903,* London, 1960, p. 193.
9.   Raymond Aron, *Paix et Guerre entre les Nations,* Paris, 1962, pp. 113ff.
10.   For a definition of the foreign policy-making elite in Britain, see D.C. Watt, *Personalities and Policies, Studies in the Formulation of British Foreign Policy in the Twentieth Century,* London and South Bend, Indiana, 1965 (reprint New York, 1976), pp. 1-15.
11.   On the Stalinist purges see Robert Conquest, *The Great Terror: Stalin's Purge of the Thirties,* London, 1968.

12. See David Caute, *The Fellow Travellers, A Postscript to the Enlightenment*, London, 1973.
13. On Willi Munzenberg see Babette Groes, *Willi Munzenberg: eine politische Biographie*, Stuttgart, 1967; also Helmut Gruber, 'Willi Muenzenberg, Propagandist for and against the Comintern', *International Review of Social History*, Vol. x, 1965.
14. See R.H. Pear, 'The Impact of the New Deal on British Economic and Political Ideas', *Bulletin of the British Association of American Studies*, New Series, No. 4, August 1962.
15. John Lukacs, *The Last European War, September 1939-December 1941*, London, 1977.
16. As argued in D.C. Watt, 'The Breakdown of the European Security System, 1930-1939', *Paper Presented to the XIV International Congress of Historical Science*, San Francisco, 1975.
17. John Erickson, *The Soviet High Command, 1918-1941*, London, 1962, pp. 470-1, 478-9, 505-6.

2 THE GERMAN GENERALS AND THE OUTBREAK OF WAR 1938-1939

Gerhardt Weinberg

While imprisoned along with other German generals and admirals after the Second World War, Field-Marshal Ritter von Leeb wrote in his diary on 10 December 1945:

> After the experiences of this war, we shall, in view of the enormous numerical superiority of the English fleet, have to give priority in a future naval construction programme to U-Boats, destroyers, mine layers . . . above all to the strongest naval air arm in order to be able to search out and destroy the English fleet in its hidden bases.[1]

Here we see a conservative and generally moderate German military leader so fastened to perceptions of a world which had vanished, that he quite automatically assumes that World War II will be followed after an appropriate interval by World War III in which Germany will fight essentially the same enemies as in the two preceding struggles but will, of course, attempt to do better by applying the lessons learned in the war that had just ended.

If one of those whose reputation as a sceptic about National Socialism was strong enough for him to be rudely retired in the house-cleaning of 4 February 1938, could express himself in the manner quoted after World War II, it should be easier to understand how completely a new conflict was thought likely, perhaps assumed inevitable, during World War I. The great debate about war aims in World War I Germany, which was almost as heated as the controversy on that subject more recently inaugurated by Fritz Fischer, had revolved around several issues, but unquestionably one key element had been the anticipation of a later war against at least some of the same enemies, England in particular, and the need to secure in any peace settlement territories and arrangements that would assure an advantageous starting situation for Germany in the next war. Certainly the discussion about the future of Belgium cannot be understood without regard for this factor.

The war, of course, ended in a manner very different from the expectations of those Germans who had confidently discussed new maps of Europe in the years 1914-18. The peace settlement both limited German military strength and reduced her territory. Of·the territorial losses, none was perceived as more horrendous than the losses to Poland. Here was a double indignity. The victors had had the effrontery to reverse Frederick the Great's corridor construction: instead of an East-West corridor connecting Prussia with Brandenburg and separating the main territory of Poland from her port of Danzig, the new settlement established a north-south corridor connecting Poland with the Baltic and separating the main territory of Germany from what had come to be called East Prussia. As if this was not bad enough, the lands Germany had lost were not handed over to a respectable state like Russia, with which Prussia had in the past traded Polish territory in very much the way children trade marbles; but adding insult to injury, the area was turned over to Poles, a group of beings perceived as hardly human, surely undeserving of the proud title of a nation, and in any case thought incapable of establishing and running a country.[2]

Although German military activities in the Weimar years were concentrated on the reconstruction of military power, domestic turmoil, and concern about possible foreign attack, there was some military planning that went beyond these preoccupations. The critical priority of all German military leaders after 1919 was the hope for recovery of lands lost to Poland; and the major line of thinking and planning was directed towards that end. The most likely prospect was thought to be a new war between Poland and the Soviet Union which would open the opportunity for joint German-Soviet efforts to make the hated country once again disappear from the map. The more remote possibility was a situation in which assurance of security to France and the worldwide preoccupations of England might free Germany from the danger of a two-front war if she attacked Poland by herself.[3]

Three aspects of this military thought need to be underlined since all played key roles in the perceptions of German generals in the 1930s as in the 1920s. The first, of course, is the fundamental assumption that war would continue to be an accepted instrument of national policy for Germany as well as for other countries. The second was the concern that Germany in the future should avoid a two-front war. Surely every effort had to be made to avoid a situation like that of 1914 where Germany had fought in the east and west simultaneously. It was assumed that if Germany were ever involved in a war in the West, Poland would try to take advantage of the situation to seize additional territory from Germany; but there was at least a slight possibility of a quiescent West if Germany attacked Poland — and if that were the situation, fighting might not be necessary. The third factor was the importance of co-operation with the Soviet Union against Poland, a co-operation that seemed to be based on national interest entirely separate from and independent of the differing social systems of the two countries, and that therefore could be expected to become operative at the appropriate moment whether or not there had been prior formal agreement.

It was into such a framework of assumptions and expectations that the National Socialist regime was subsumed by the leaders of the German army. When Hitler explained to them a few days after assuming the chancellorship that his government would crush democracy, pacifism, and Marxism at home, build up a vast military establishment, and then use the new army for the conquest and Germanisation of living space in Eastern Europe, the generals were on the whole not unfavourably impressed.[4] There was not much in Hitler's domestic policies as explained to them to which the military leaders objected: the idea of rebuilding German military might appealed to them greatly, and they associated the idea of conquering living space in the East with the recapture of lands lost to Poland together with perhaps such additional parts of Poland as might be obtainable in the next partition of that degenerate country. After all, Prussia had once held substantial territories beyond the 1914 border, even if only briefly, and there had been much discussion of the need to annex smaller or larger pieces beyond the 1914 border during the First World War.[5]

In this alignment of the military leaders with Hitler there were several miscalculations, mostly on the side of the soldiers; and it would take some of them years to recognise those miscalculations — while the rest never figured them out at all. The first misunderstanding was about the location of the living space in the East that Hitler intended to conquer. While the generals assumed Poland, Hitler wanted such vast stretches that they could only be taken from Russia. Since in Hitler's view, Poland was only a subsidiary element in the picture, he could contemplate and actually sign a temporary agreement with that country — an idea repugnant to his military (and diplomatic) advisers in whose thinking hostility to Poland was a central and fixed, not a minor and subordinate consideration. They could only grit their teeth over the German-Polish agreement of January 1934, but they certainly did not alter their beliefs. (It was not until Hitler decided to attack Russia that they learned that he had not changed *his* beliefs either.)

A second misunderstanding arose from Hitler's attitude towards the Reichswehr. As became dramatically evident in June 1934, Hitler decided to forestall any idea of a politicised party army of the sort

Ernst Röhm and some other SA leaders preferred by quite literally beheading that organisation. The highest leaders of the army were implicated in these murders, prepared to pay the price of criminal complicity for what they imagined was their own and their country's advantage. In reality this was a complete miscalculation. Hitler was in a hurry, needed an army to fight soon, and therefore wanted to keep and use the existing leadership — while looking forward to doing slowly and with precision what Röhm hoped to accomplish swiftly and with boisterous celebrations. In this regard, as in the closely related sphere of economic and social structure, Hitler's triumph over what *others* perceived as the radicals among the Nazis was in reality the victory of the most extreme radical concepts over ideas of change that were still essentially within a traditional framework.[6] Hitler's preparations for *his* kind of army were quite small in peacetime and only accelerated once war had started; in the meantime he was as voluble in his assurances to the soldiers as to the Poles, and equally sincere.

The appearance of a maintained traditional military structure and leadership served to reconcile the military commanders even if some had qualms about the methods used. The murder of the wife of General von Schleicher caused hardly a stir — in POW camps after the war Field-Marshals von Leeb and von List were still hysterical about the shame von Blomberg had allegedly brought on the army.[7] In the early years of the National Socialist regime, therefore, real enthusiasm, cautious professionalism, and determined blindness reigned supreme among the generals. Officers who began by turning their 'non-Aryan' comrades out of the army in 1934 would end up by turning their politically compromised comrades over to the hangman ten years later.[8] In the mid-1930s, the first of these processes had been completed, but there were as yet no candidates for the second.

With the one-war contingency that German military men had been concerned about — a war with Poland — temporarily removed from the scene by diplomacy, the build-up of the German armed forces moved forward along lines most of the soldiers favoured. There were arguments over the proper speed of expansion as well as over problems of equipment, personnel assignment, and tactical doctrine; but none of this went beyond the usual daily frictions that accompany major change in the size of a military establishment. More severe friction, and friction having a bearing on the contingency of war, would grow out of the conflict over the respective roles of the army general staff and the staff of the War Minister and Commander-in-Chief of the Armed Forces.

During the years of the Weimar Republic, the problem of how Ger-

many's military forces were to be directed as a whole was never satis-
factorily solved, but the issue was not of great importance. The navy
had managed to secure considerable independence for itself; and
personal continuity on the inside as well as diffidence about naval
matters on the outside protected some of this status in the National
Socialist period. Personal and political factors performed the same role
for the new air force. Hermann Göring was made air minister as well
as commander-in-chief of the air force, and his personal closeness to
Hitler guaranteed that the air force would be effectively independent of
any military command structure below the chief of state himself.

The importance of the independence of the navy and air force will
be seen in the impact of the attempt to establish a central, overall
command structure upon the relationship between that structure and
the command and general staff of the army.[9] As first General Walther
von Reichenau and, after 1 October 1935, General Wilhelm Keitel,
together with his chief assistant Alfred Jodl, attempted to create an
armed forces command structure in the office of the Minister of War,
there was a direct clash between them and the commander-in-chief and
the chief-of-staff of the army. Given the independence of the navy and
the air force, the developing 'Armed Forces Office' (*Wehrmachtamt*)
with its 'National Defence Section' (*Abteilung Landesvertaidigung*)
threatened to become a sort of competing army general staff at a higher
level. In von Reichenau's time, the conflict was muted; but his successors, the team of Keitel and Jodl, moved forward rapidly, enthusias-
tically and abrasively.[10]

They not only wanted to assume the role of staff planners for all the
armed forces in theory and for the army in practice, but they saw the
role of such a staff in a new and different way. The general staff tradition of the Prussian and then German army had insisted on a major
advisory role in broad strategic-political matters. The risks to be run,
the basic nature of military deployment, and at times even the details
of foreign policy had been considered within the proper sphere of
general staff advice, if not direction.[11] If there had at times been a ten-
dency, most recently personified by Erich Ludendorff, towards military
control of decisions that were properly political, the orientation of
Keitel and Jodl was in the opposite direction. Personally fascinated by
Hitler and impressed by the dynamism of his movement, they now
wanted the military to operate as a purely executive arm of the Führer;
they would merely translate his commands as transmitted by the
Minister of War into formal military directives, the more detailed elab-
oration of which could then be left to the separate general staffs of the

branches of the armed forces. No one along the route, neither they themselves nor most assuredly the staffs of the army, navy or air force, had any business giving advice about the wisdom or unwisdom of the orders given. If Hitler with the *Führerprinzip*, the leadership principle, had transferred the rule of absolute obedience to superior orders from the infantry company to the political arena, they now wanted it returned to the military establishment at the very top. That in this attempt they would clash with an army leadership insisting on its own responsibility to give advice and weigh risks, and that they would find themselves in full accord with Hitler's preferences, should not be surprising.[12]

When the first outline for a German surprise attack on Czechoslovakia had gone in 1935 from the Armed Forces Office over War Minister von Blomberg's signature to the high command of the army, the army chief-of-staff, General Ludwig Beck, had rejected the whole idea and simply refused to work on it.[13] It was then, and continued to be, his judgement that any such attack would lead to a general war which Germany must lose. In June 1937, the Armed Forces Office once again prepared and von Blomberg issued an over-all plan for the employment of Germany's armed forces, and once again this caused difficulties.[14] Since von Blomberg and his staff had not consulted the army on the basic issue of the risks involved, Beck once again disregarded much of the new directive,[15] and the commander-in-chief of the army, General von Fritsch, went in person to the Armed Forces Office to complain.[16]

The arguments continued through the summer and autumn of 1937. Though he made a friendly visit to Paris in June 1937, Beck thought of France as Germany's most likely and most dangerous enemy.[17] He was, however, opposed to Germany's taking the risk of any war which was likely to become general, and this meant in effect though not in theory to practically any war started by Germany at all. The problem of those risks and the probability of incurring them was, of course, in the background of the controversy as Keitel and Jodl argued for their position of unquestioning implementation of whatever inspiration the leader of Germany might pass on to his soldiers. While the argument among the latter over command structure was still in progress, Hitler summoned the highest figures in the Reich to a conference at which he voiced the inspirations he wanted implemented.

When Hitler met the Minister of War, the Foreign Minister, and the chiefs of the three branches of the armed forces on 5 November 1937, he gave his assessment of the current situation and his plans for the

future as far as he cared to reveal them.[18] Germany, he asserted, needed
space for her population which could not be fed from her present space.
Dependence on world trade would not do; it limited independence and
was in any case dubious in a world in which all countries were indus-
trialising.[19] Germany would have to expand by seizing agriculturally
useful land. This would involve war, and Germany had to decide where
to seize the most with the least risk. Force alone could solve Germany's
problem, and the only questions to be answered were 'where and how?'

In his discussion of the possible answers to these questions, Hitler
threw together two types of consideration: the short-term one of
'improving our military-political situation' which required the conquest
of Austria and Czechoslovakia, and the long-term one of 'solving the
German space problem'. The short-term task would help with the bigger
one; troops freed by better borders and the additional divisions
recruited in the annexed territories as well as the economic resources of
the seized lands would strengthen Germany for its subsequent war.

Hitler argued that the effort to reach the long-term goal would have
to be launched by 1943-5. Thereafter the odds would shift against
Germany; but the short-term goal might be reached much earlier, and
Hitler gave a great deal of attention to the prospects for that. In the dis-
cussion which followed, von Blomberg and von Fritsch argued that
Britain and France might not stay out of a war Germany started in
Central Europe, and that Germany was not ready to face them. Von
Neurath expressed doubts about Hitler's expectation of a war between
Italy and the Western Powers in the Mediterranean. Hitler maintained
his own position; but when von Fritsch suggested that in view of what
had been said he ought not to go through with his intended leave, Hitler
responded that the probability of war was not that close.

No one argued at the meeting with the Führer's long-term aims. With
his short-term aims, no-one argued either; all the objections dealt with
his calculations as to the risks involved. What Beck in his subsequent
analysis of the record of this meeting, as well as von Blomberg, von
Fritsch, and von Neurath, criticised was the assessment by Hitler that
England and France would stay out of a war Germany might start in
Central Europe.[20] Beck, furthermore, was appalled at the whole line of
reasoning which led Hitler to conclude that war was necessary, but this
view was not shared by any of those present.[21]

There have been efforts to interpret away the record of this meeting
or to pretend that Hitler's comments were unimportant or meaningless.
Such efforts are irrelevant for understanding German military planning
since none of those present at the meeting or immediately informed of

Hitler's wishes could possibly know that there ever would be such a literature; they were too busy trying to carry out what they took to be the dictator's orders.

Göring immediately gave some new directives to the general staff of the air force. A new general construction plan for the navy reflecting the decisions of 5 November took a few weeks to prepare; it was issued on 21 December.[22] Both to assure a uniform approach by all branches of the armed forces — when each was working on its own implementing procedures — and in accordance with their concept of the military being purely an instrument and never an adviser of the political leader, Keitel and Jodl now prepared a supplement to the general war directive of 24 June.[23] Von Blomberg's agreement to this approach, in spite of his reservations at the 5 November meeting, may well have been caused by his eagerness to utilise an expression of Hitler's will to override all objections in the high command of the army to such general directives. They might object to them when issued on von Blomberg's own authority; once the revision of his order had been approved by Hitler, it could not be resisted without an open break with the Führer himself.[24] The revision was accordingly prepared in the Armed Forces Office, approved by Hitler, and issued like the navy's new programme on 21 December 1937.[25]

The prior directive of June had left open the possibility of 'military exploitation of politically favourable opportunities'; the new formulation called for an 'aggressive war against Czechoslovakia'. Hitler had picked his immediate goal and alerted his generals, but he would move forward as opportunity offered.

While Hitler watched for opportunities, and nudged the process a bit too, the occasion to make drastic changes among his military and diplomatic advisers arose, with at least some help from Hitler himself, early in 1938. On 12 January the German Minister of War and Commander-in-Chief of the Armed Forces, Field-Marshal Werner von Blomberg, married a young woman who turned out to have a record of moral offences. Hitler seized the opportunity to rid himself of a whole series of generals and diplomats and to take over the position of Commander-in-Chief of the Armed Forces himself. The details of what has come to be known as the Fritsch-Blomberg crisis need not be recounted here, but one aspect of it would have a most important bearing on the situation of Germany's military leadership: the succession at the top.[26]

Almost as soon as von Blomberg's 'fault' was called to Hitler's attention, and before anyone had an opportunity to discuss the matter with him, he decided to dismiss von Blomberg and also to use trumped-up charges of homosexuality, that he knew to be false, to dismiss von Fritsch as Commander-in-Chief of the Army. What has often been ignored in the literature on this crisis is that Hitler was perfectly willing to tolerate in his associates and officials all sorts of defects far more serious than the real or imagined ones of the two general officers, and that the man appointed to succeed one of them was known by Hitler to be vulnerable to questions about *his* marriage.

If Hitler acted so quickly in the cases of von Blomberg and von Fritsch, therefore, it makes no sense to attribute those hurried actions to the Führer's disappointment in von Blomberg or his initial belief in the charges against von Fritsch. Quite the contrary, Hitler promptly utilised what looked like wonderful excuses to get rid of these two under circumstances almost guaranteed to weaken any independence left to the military and to strengthen his own position. The peculiar advantage of the supposed faults of the two generals, from Hitler's point of view, was that a strong reaction from the army leadership was practically precluded as long as the sordid circumstances of the whole operation could be kept concealed, a problem Hitler dealt with by arranging for a succession with a vested interest in keeping it concealed. Before the succession is examined, some further aspects of the dismissals must be mentioned.

Von Blomberg's marriage left him without support from his colleagues; he had enjoyed little enough before because he was seen as an advocate of National Socialist influence in the army. In any case, as a devoted admirer of Hitler, he could be depended upon to go quietly. Von Fritsch, though not uncritical, was equally unwilling to do anything himself or to encourage those among the military who were inclined to act forcefully on behalf of a leader they admired and in whose downfall they sensed, even before they fully understood, a foul manoeuvre. In October 1926, when General Hans von Seeckt had been removed quite legally from a position equivalent to the one von Fritsch held now, the latter, then a lieutenant-colonel, had urged von Seeckt to use force against the government of the Weimar Republic in order to maintain himself in office.[27] He would not move himself now. In a way, von Fritsch continued to believe in Hitler as he had never been willing to support the Republic.

Given this loyalty to Hitler of the men removed, why did he drop them? It is too often forgotten that von Blomberg was not originally chosen by Hitler himself, but by President Paul von Hindenburg.[28] Though the appointment had been acceptable to Hitler, and though von

Blomberg had proved himself a willing and capable instrument of Hitler's will, he retained some independence, a quality he had shown in the conference of 5 November. Von Fritsch was even more obviously a man out of tune with Hitler's preferences. Like von Blomberg, he had been the choice of von Hindenburg when Hitler and von Blomberg himself would have preferred to appoint von Reichenau.[29] Unlike von Blomberg, he had demonstrated a certain rigidity in resisting accommodation to the regime, and this had been recalled to Hitler not only on 5 November but also at a subsequent meeting of von Fritsch with Hitler on 9 November.[30] Now that Hitler felt ready to begin implementing the aggressive policies he intended to pursue, he wanted not just willing instruments but totally dependent and pliant tools.

This raises the key issue of the succession to von Blomberg and von Fritsch. Hitler decided to take the position of Commander-in-Chief of the Armed Forces himself and to use as his staff in that capacity the staff Keitel had been building up.[31] Hitler's daily contacts with Keitel during the crisis convinced him that here was a man he could depend on, a judgement that correctly assessed an officer who would remain in the same position until 1945. In this case, as in so many others, Hitler displayed an almost uncanny ability to sense the presence (or absence) of absolute devotion to himself. As a replacement for von Fritsch Hitler wanted to appoint his favourite among the generals, Walther von Reichenau. Keitel managed to dissuade Hitler by pointing to von Reichenau's failings in the one and only field where Keitel could detect mortal sin: von Reichenau was neither hard-working nor thorough. Furthermore, Keitel — whose objections to von Reichenau were supported for entirely different reasons by others — had a candidate who was likely to meet Hitler's needs even if Hitler did not know him well as yet.

Walther von Brauchitsch was technically competent, had enough seniority to calm the army leadership, and was politically pliable. Before receiving the appointment — which a man of minimal decency would have refused except on an acting basis at a time when the charges against von Fritsch were still to be tried — von Brauchitsch had to promise to bring the army 'closer to the state and its ideology'; to make a host of personnel changes, and a string of other concessions.[32]

Hitler was quickly, and correctly, convinced that in von Brauchitsch he had found the man he needed. Here was an individual so hopelessly compromised that Hitler would always be able to bend him to his will. About to resign from the army because of marital problems when the big prize dangled before his eyes, von Brauchitsch needed and received the assurance of financial support from Hitler to enable him to get out of his first into a second marriage.[33] If the dependence on Hitler created by this secret subvention was not enough, the new Commander-in-Chief of the army turned out to be an anatomical marvel, a man totally without a backbone, who would be the despair of all who hoped for some sign of strength and leadership from him in the crises ahead. In the critical years when Hitler wanted to attack Czechoslovakia, when he attacked Poland, and when he expanded the war in the north, the west, the south-east, and finally the east, the Commander-in-Chief of the German army was a slavish servant of the Führer. Here is perhaps the single most important factor in the internal German military situation before the war and during its critical first years.[34]

An instructive comparison might be made between King Edward VIII and von Brauchitsch: to marry the woman he loved one gave up his throne, the other sold his soul to the devil. And on the instalment plan. The down-payment had been a condition of von Brauchitsch's initial appointment and has already been discussed, but there were to be further instalments, more or less parallel to the monthly payments to von Brauchitsch's now divorced first wife. As Hitler diverted attention from the domestic crisis to foreign affairs by speeding up the annexation of Austria, he did *not* have to worry about the army; with no danger of foreign intervention, even Beck was quite willing to throw together a quick plan for the occupation of that country. As Hitler moved towards war on Czechoslovakia, however, the situation changed.

Although the work on new draft directives for the German army in early May 1938 was deliberately kept secret from the army general staff,[35] there was enough discussion of the intent to attack within the highest levels of the German government to alert Beck.[36] On 7 May he handed von Brauchitsch a memorandum for Hitler arguing that an attack on Czechoslovakia would start a general war that Germany must lose and accurately predicting the strategy Britain and France would follow.[37] Von Brauchitsch took this to Keitel before showing it to Hitler; and since Keitel was actually working on new plans for an attack on Czechoslovakia on Hitler's instructions, he advised von Brauchitsch to present only the strictly military portion of Beck's memorandum to Hitler.[38] Von Brauchitsch followed this advice when he saw Hitler on or about 12 May. Hitler rejected all Beck's views; he was himself already determined to attack Czechoslovakia that year and was confident that there would be an isolated war in which the Western Powers would not intervene.[39] Later that month, he explained his views to this effect to an assemblage of military leaders.

The difference in assessment between Hitler and many of the
generals would continue from early May to late September 1938. Hitler
operated on the assumption that extensive construction and noise about
the construction of fortifications in the West would isolate Czechoslovakia militarily, while propaganda about the Sudeten Germans would
isolate her diplomatically so that there could be a localised war. A number of the generals were sceptical about the military adequacy of the
former and the political adequacy of the latter procedure. In the event,
neither was put to the test.[40]

The errors in both Hitler's political calculation of an isolated war and
in the tactical directives for such an operation were pointed out by
Beck in several memoranda.[41] The attempt to enlist von Brauchitsch in
holding Hitler back failed completely; when Hitler needed his new
minion to restore confidence in himself among the generals after the
foul treatment accorded the revered von Fritsch and also to rally them
for the projected war against Czechoslovakia, von Brauchitsch readily
complied. At the meeting of Hitler and von Brauchitsch with many of
the generals on 13 June, von Brauchitsch told those assembled of the
forthcoming attack on Czechoslovakia, with which he fully identified
himself, as an introduction to Hitler's presentation of a carefully doc-
tored account of the Fritsch case.[42] Having thus expressed his own
support for Hitler's handling of both the internal and the foreign policy
issues facing the regime, von Brauchitsch turned a deaf ear to Beck's
further pleadings. Instead of the general strike of the generals that
Beck recommended, these efforts merely led to Beck's own resignation.[43] As Sir Lewis Namier has commented, 'Sense, courage, and
character cannot be transmitted from him who has them to him who
has not.'[44] If von Brauchitsch sided with Hitler out of a combination of
cowardice and inclination, Keitel and Jodl took the same view out of
enthusiastic conviction.[45]

In these circumstances, military planning for the attack on
Czechoslovakia went forward. If Hitler had his ideas for isolating
the war, some of his generals had theirs for preventing it. They would
urge the British to remain firm, operating on the widely held view of
the time that a clear British warning might have averted the war of
1914. On the other hand, they also prepared a coup against Hitler if he
ordered the attack all the same. The details of these contacts and pro-
jects cannot be reviewed here.[46] Four aspects are, however, important
for our understanding of the German generals in the face of a possible
war. First, the whole idea of a war against and about Czechoslovakia,
and one in which Poland might even be on Germany's side, was entirely

outside the military tradition of the Prussian and German general staff.[47] Second, there was a widely held view, shared by the new chief of staff of the army, General Franz Halder, that a general war would develop out of any German attack on Czechoslovakia; that such a general war would see the reconstitution of the world alliance against Germany of World War I — including eventually the United States and the Soviet Union — and that Germany was certain to lose such a war. Third, that if Hitler was warned of this contingency by both his military advisers and the British, he might desist from ordering the attack; but fourth, that if he ordered it anyway in the face of such warnings, an attempt to overthrow his government should be prepared.

In the final evolution of the Czech crisis, in the face of an English warning delivered at the last moment, in view of clear signs of a reluctant German public, and with Mussolini urging a conference, Hitler backed off, settling at the Munich conference for his ostensible and propagandistically defensible rather than his real aims.

Speculation on what would have happened had Hitler gone forward with the order to attack Czechoslovakia is not especially profitable; my reading of the evidence suggests that Britain and France would have gone to war but that in the face of von Brauchitsch's dubious position,[48] the planned coup would either have been called off or misfired. More important than such theoretical constructs are the real effects of the September crisis on Hitler and his generals. Hitler had backed down; he not only regretted having done so to the last days of his life, but in the immediately following months combined a projection of the show of weakness on his own part with a determination to avoid any repetition.

The first of these was simple enough: he would berate those military and diplomatic advisers who had warned of a general war for showing a despicable and unwarranted weakness of will. Not a single one among them appears to have mustered the nerve to respond that it was Hitler who had backed down and funked putting their dire predictions to the test of action. On the contrary, in their relief over the avoidance of the predicted disasters, they meekly accepted the charge of cowardice and resolved not to expose themselves to such charges next time.

Since Hitler was determined not to be cheated out of a war, that next time was not to be long in coming. He assured a group of high-ranking officers to this effect on 10 February 1939,[49] and discussed the whole subject at length in his famous talk to the generals on 23 May.[50] In that speech he also alluded to the two points which, combined with von Brauchitsch's subservience and the distorted impressions of the 1938 crisis, would make the generals willing to move without much question and even with a little enthusiasm in 1939. In the first place, the enemy now was to be Poland. Here was a country that deserved invasion; as Quartermaster-General Eduard Wagner — who would commit suicide in July 1944 lest he betray the names of associates in the 20 July plot — wrote to his wife on 31 August 1939: 'wir freuen uns offen gestanden darauf' — we admit to looking forward to it gladly.[51] Secondly, Hitler hinted at a possible agreement with the Soviet Union.[52] Here was a perspective that to the highest military leaders of Germany looked positively dazzling: Hitler coming back after five years to the very view they had held since 1920, namely co-operation with Russia to destroy Poland, and all this with the lovely prospect of a one-front war.

It is in this context that one must, in my judgement, examine the reaction of most German generals to Hitler's explanation to them on 22 August not only of his decision to attack Poland after signing an agreement with the Soviet Union, but his determination under no circumstances to allow a repetition of 1938.[53] His reference to the fact that the only thing he feared was that some 'Schweinehund', some SOB would come along at the last minute with a compromise to avoid war was obviously a reference to Neville Chamberlain; and those present were clear in their own minds — even if some pretended otherwise under oath later — that Hitler wanted war.[54]

The ever faithful von Brauchitsch would not even reply to a warning letter from Beck;[55] Halder agreed to see his predecessor, but would not budge either.[56] That General George Thomas's last-minute attempts to discourage *his* superior, General Keitel, would produce no effect on that devotee of the Führer will surprise no one.[57] Only with the Abwehr, the military intelligence apparatus, were there doubts; the critical command positions in the German army, however, were filled by men who were either satisfied with the developments or not sufficiently worried to do anything other than play their part in launching the war that would destroy so much. They were not all as confident as Hitler that the West would stay out,[58] though the evidence suggests that Hitler was himself fully prepared to risk Western intervention at the end; but eagerness for war on Poland and relief over the agreement with Russia were strong enough to still most doubts. There was no German public rejoicing in September 1939 to match that of August 1914, but the *Burgfrieden,* the harmony within, that had quietened political debate in 1914 did indeed return, if only for a short time, to the one place where it counted in the Germany of 1939: the high command of the German army.

Notes

1. Georg Meyer (ed.), *Generalfieldmarschall Ritter von Leeb, Tagebuchauf-zeichnungen und Lagebeurteilungen aus zwei Weltkriegen*, Stuttgart, Deutsche Verlags-Anstalt, 1976 (hereafter cited as *Leeb Papers*), p. 80. n. 195.
2. A useful recent study of German attitudes and images is Harry K. Rosenthal, *German and Pole: National Conflict and Modern Myth*, Gaines-ville, University Press of Florida, 1976.
3. There is as yet no comprehensive study of German military planning in the Weimar years. The best summary available is in Gaines Post, Jr., *The Civil-Military Fabric of Weimar Foreign Policy*, Princeton, Princeton University Press, 1973. Important on the naval side is Carl-Axel Gemzell, *Raeder, Hitler und Skandinavien, Der Kampf für einen maritimen Operationsplan*, Lund, Gleerup, 1965.
4. There is a full account in Gerhard L. Weinberg, *The Foreign Policy of Hitler's Germany, Diplomatic Revolution in Europe, 1933-1936*, Chicago, University of Chicago Press, 1970, pp. 26-7.
5. On this subject, see Imanuel Geiss, *Der Polnische Grenzstreifen, 1914-1918*, Lübeck/Hamburg, Matthiesen, 1960.
6. For a clear statement of this view on the nature of National Socialism and the extreme radicalism of Hitler as opposed to the far less revolutionary character of the National Socialist 'left-wing', see Henry A. Turner, Jr., 'Fascism and Modernisation', in H.A. Turner (ed.), *Reappraisals of Fascism*, New York, Franklin Watts, 1975, pp. 120-2.
7. *Leeb Papers*, pp. 78-9.
8. A thoughtful analysis of the application of the 'Aryan Paragraph' to the army is in Klaus-Jürgen Müller, *Das Heer und Hitler, Armee und national-sozialistisches Regime 1933-1940*, Stuttgart, Deutsche Verlags-Anstalt, 1969, pp. 78-86.
9. The best survey in ibid., ch. 5.
10. The first author to recognise the relationship of this organisational issue to policy questions was Gemzell, but the matter is most clearly discussed by Müller.
11. Gordon Craig, *The Politics of the Prussian Army, 1640-1945*, New York, Oxford University Press, 1956.
12. It should be noted that although there was a short clash between Hitler and Jodl in the autumn of 1942, Keitel and Jodl both retained Hitler's confi-dence until 1945, a confidence they more than fully reciprocated.
13. Weinberg, *Foreign Policy*, p. 224.
14. The 'Weisung 1937/38' of 24 June 1937 is in International Military Tri-bunal, *Trial of the Major War Criminals*, Nürnberg, IMT, 1946-48 (hereafter cited as *TMWC*), 34, 733-45.
15. Wolfgang Foerster, *Ein General kämpft gegen den Krieg, Aus den nach-gelassenen Papieren des Generalstabschefs Ludwig Beck*, Munich, Munchener-Dom Verlag, 1949, p. 63.
16. Nürnberg document 1781-PS, National Archives.
17. On Beck's visit to Paris, see Müller, pp. 634-5; Foerster, pp. 47-9; Hans Speidel (ed.), *Ludwig Beck, Studien*, Stuttgart, K.F. Koehler, 1955, pp. 295-302.

18. The memorandum of Friedrich Hossbach on the meeting is printed in *Documents on German Foreign Policy, 1918-1945*, Series D. k No. 19, and in *TMWC*, 25, 403-13; a supplementary statement by Hossbach is in *TMWC*, 42, 222-30. An important source is Hossbach's memoirs, *Zwischen Wehrmacht und Hitler*, Wolfenbüttel, Wolfenbütteler Verlags-anstalt, 1949.

19. This was an old theme of Hitler's, see Gerhard L. Weinberg (ed.), *Hitlers zweites Buch*, Stuttgart, Deutsche Verlags-Anstalt, 1961, p. 60 and n. 1.

20. Beck was shown the memorandum by Hossbach himself since he was acting in von Fritsch's place during the latter's leave. Beck's memorandum is in Bundesarchiv, H 08-28/4, item 52.

21. Admiral Raeder said nothing in the first part of the meeting of 5 November. Since his memoirs and his testimony at Nürnberg are wholly unreliable, one can only assume that he – as usual – was in general agreement with Hitler.

22. Jost Dülffer, *Weimar, Hitler und die Marine, Reichspolitik und Flottenbau 1920-1939*, Dusseldorf, Droste, 1973, p. 455.

23. Müller, pp. 246-7.

24. This probably explains the absence of a reaction by Beck; he was not yet psychologically ready for an open break with Hitler.

25. *TMWC*, 28, 356, 745-7; *Documents on German Foreign Policy*, D, 7, 547-51.

26. Müller, ch. 6, is useful, but the author has been misled by too narrow a focus on the details without proper regard for the general pattern of Hitler's conduct. The account of Harold C. Deutsch, *Hitler and His Generals, the Hidden Crisis, January-June 1938*, Minneapolis, University of Minnesota Press, 1974, is both the most detailed and the most reliable.

27. Friedrich von Rabenau, *Seeckt, Aus seinem Leben, 1918-1936*, Leipzig, Hase and Koehler, 1940, p. 536.

28. Müller, pp. 49-50; Deutsch, pp. 8-10.

29. Deutsch, pp. 11-13.

30. Ibid., pp. 29-30, 71, 74-5.

31. Ibid., p. 119

32. Müller, pp. 263-4. For an example of how the promise of von Brauchitsch to dismiss inconvenient generals was implemented, see *Leeb Papers*, pp. 41-2.

33. Deutsch, ch. 7, has a full account. I am indebted to Professor Deutsch for personal explanations supplementing his book.

34. See Hildegard von Kotze (ed.), *Heeresadjutant bei Hitler, 1938-1943, Aufzeichungen des Majors Engel*, Stuttgart, Deutsche Verlags-Anstalt, 1974, 28 March 1938, p. 19; 18 October 1938, p. 42, and especially 20 August 1941, pp. 109-10, where Hitler berated von Brauchitsch about his marriage problems in front of subordinate officers.

35. Walter Görlitz (ed.), *Generalfeldmarschall Keitel, Verbrecher oder Offizier?* Göttingen, Musterschmidt, 1961 (hereafter cited as Keitel Papers), p. 183; Müller, p. 300.

36. Müller, p. 301; *TMWC*, 37, 443-60.

37. Müller, pp. 302-5; Foerster, pp. 81-7.

38. *Keitel Papers*, p. 184.

39. The author will explain the sequence of events in April-May 1938 in considerable detail in a forthcoming book on German foreign policy, 1937-1939, to be published by the University of Chicago Press.

40. As for the fortifications, Hitler simply transferred control of that work to his favourite builder of the day, Fritz Todt. In September, he would boast about the great accomplishments in this regard in public right after he had

been warned privately of their inadequacy by General Wilhelm Adam.

41. The text of the 29 May memorandum is in Bundesarchiv, H 08-28/3, parts published in Foerster, pp. 90-4; cf. Müller, pp. 309-13. The 3 June memorandum is in Müller, pp. 651-4.

42. Deutsch, pp. 401-6.

43. Müller, pp. 317-33.

44. *In the Nazi Era*, London, Macmillan, 1952, p. 32.

45. Note Jodl's comment in his diary, *TMWC*, 28, 373.

46. There is an account in Müller, ch. 8. Professor Deutsch is preparing a volume devoted to the subject. It is treated in chapter 11 of my forthcoming book on German foreign policy, 1937-1939.

47. Fighting in Bohemia in the Napoleonic and the German civil wars was always a part of wider conflicts, with the location a purely coincidental element. In the Weimar years, concern about Czechoslovakia was always subsidiary to worries about France and Poland; see, in addition to the book by Post, F. Gregory Campbell, *Confrontation in Central Europe, Weimar Germany and Czechoslovakia*, Chicago, University of Chicago Press, 1975.

48. Professor Deutsch speculates that von Brauchitsch would 'conceivably' have gone along with a coup: *The Conspiracy against Hitler in the Twilight War*, Minneapolis, University of Minnesota Press, 1968, p. 38. On the general problem of the diffidence of the opposition to Hitler, George K. Romoser's article, 'The Politics of Uncertainty: The German Resistance Movement', *Social Research*, 31, No. 1, Spring, 1964, 73-93, is still very useful.

49. Helmut Krausnick and Harold C. Deutsch (eds.), *Helmuth Grosscurth, Tagebücher eines Abwehroffiziers 1938-1940*, Stuttgart, Deutsche Verlags-Anstalt, 1970, p. 166.

50. *Documents on Germany Foreign Policy*, D 6, No. 433.

51. Elisabeth Wagner (ed.), *Der Generalquartiermeister*, Munich, Olzog, 1963 (hereafter cited as *Wagner Papers*), p. 109.

52. The author has reviewed this subject in *Germany and the Soviet Union, 1939-1941*, Leyden, Brill, 1954 and 1972), chs. 2-4; it will be placed in the general context of German foreign policy in the author's forthcoming book.

53. Wagner, ironically, thought that this might be possible: first an agreement truncating Poland under German threats, and then a second stage in the spring of 1940 when Germany and Russia would jointly crush the remaining Polish state: Wagner diary, 29 August 1939, *Wagner Papers*, p. 105. The 22 August speech has been analysed, and the various existing versions explained, by Winfrid Baumgart; the subject is reviewed in the author's forthcoming book.

54. See von Leeb's 3 October 1939 diary entry on a conversation with von Brauchitsch: 'We soldiers know from the conference at the Obersalzberg that Hitler wanted this war.' *Leeb Papers*, p. 184.

55. Hans Berod Gisevius, *Bis zum bittern Ende*, Zurich, Fretz and Wasmuth, 1946, 2, 116.

56. Ibid., p. 117.

57. An account is included in Thomas's short memoirs, 'Gedanken und Ereignisse', *Schweizer Monatschefte*, 25, December 1945, 537-58.

58. Note Wagner diary for 24 August 1939 (*Wagner Papers*, p. 93) with its report on Halder's talk to the staff officers stressing that it was Hitler who did not believe that the attack on Poland would lead to a two-front war.

3 LA GUERRE DE LONGUE DURÉE: SOME REFLECTIONS ON FRENCH STRATEGY AND DIPLOMACY IN THE 1930s

Robert Young

That summer they departed for the front, the soldiers of 1914. Before leaving the Gare de l'Est they had promised sweethearts, and mothers, and the waiters at the local brasserie that they would be home in time for Christmas. It was to be a cakewalk, a little adventure, followed by tours of a defeated and dejected Berlin. They were to be rudely deceived, these men of 1914, though it took the lives of a million and a half *poilus* before that bubble of a short, swift war was blown away for ever. In the twenty years that ensued after the Versailles peace, the famous twenty-year truce, the folly of 1914 remained to haunt the survivors, a cruel joke which evoked little laughter. The short European wars of the 1860s were now all but forgotten, fodder fit only for historians. The present had taken on a new and terrible cast — and the future as well, so far as anyone could tell. War was now to be measured in years, not in weeks or months, and by industrial machinery, raw material stockpiles, railway rolling stock, civil defence squads, and a state-supervised labour force. It no longer required great insight to see that war had become too serious a business to be left entirely to the generals, and only a wilful perversity to deny it. As Professor Watt has reminded us, historians too often forget that those in the post-war period not only lived after the war but indeed had lived through it.[1] What war had revealed of itself after 1914 had come with all the force, all the terror, of Paul's encounter on the road to Damascus.

This we sometimes overlook, thereby opening ourselves to Voltaire's acid wit. History can indeed play some very cruel tricks on the dead. For instance, the French army of 1914 certainly did anticipate a short and decisive campaign, *de brève durée,* as did its counterparts elsewhere in Europe. The soldiers were quite wrong, of course, as wrong as men can ever be. Yet their passion for dynamic warfare, for those heroic smash and grab offensive tactics, along with their eventual triumph in 1918, have led us to treat their failure of conception with the kind of forgiving hand which victors seem to require.[2] Not so for the French commanders of 1940, men whose ultimate failure was so complete that it must for ever frustrate the appetite of even the most revision-bent

41

scholar. However, or so it seems to me, their conception of the war that
awaited them, that which erupted in the autumn of 1939, was far from
being as silly and ill-founded as we are accustomed to being told.
Indeed, their comprehension of that war, their grasp of its dimensions
and its implications, was far closer to the truth than that of their more
renowned predecessors in 1914. Although clearly they did not foresee
the sudden collapse of France — in which lies their ultimate failure —
they certainly did envisage the unfolding of a long war, one of global
proportions, like the one that ended not in 1940 but rather in 1945.
Now it may well be true, indeed it is, that we could hardly have expected less from commanders who had experienced first-hand the
protracted war of 1914-18. For would we not find serious fault with
men who chose to disregard all that had been experienced, all that had
been learned, in that great and terrible war? Doubtless we would. Yet
are we not that same historical jury that has heard, and so often
affirmed, the cunning charge that generals are forever preparing for
one war by preparing in fact for the last? What we are doing, however,
is deriding the historical hindsight of the interwar generals, on the basis
of what we have learned since 1940 — in this case a hindsight which,
curiously, we now take to be beyond reproach. Sometimes, Monsieur
Voltaire, it is not only the dead we need worry about.

The subject which I address here is twofold. Simply expressed, what
can be said of the relationship between French foreign policy in the
1930s and French military policy, between those who directed French
diplomacy and those who were in command of the French armed
forces? I have tried to develop a single vehicle which I believe may be
useful for any discussion of French diplomacy and military policy. The
vehicle is the idea of a long war, an idea which the French were
obliged to embrace following the prolongation of the war in 1914 and
upon which their grand strategy in the interwar period was securely
founded. Here is an idea, a theme as it were, which should bring together the two critical dimensions of the French effort to both prevent
and prepare for the outbreak of a new war with Germany: the civilian
dimension, with particular reference to foreign policy; the military
dimension, with particular reference to the strategic appreciations of the
general staff.

Throughout the interwar period French military and civilian leadership clung unhappily to two central assumptions, facts as far as they
were concerned. First, the German problem was quite unresolved, a
judgement which the Versailles settlement seemed to have confirmed
rather than contradicted. On the one hand, France had been denied the

kind of security guarantees that had been contemplated by both
Premier Clemenceau and Marshal Foch. On the other, all the signs were
that Germany under the new Weimar Republic remained unrepentant,
bent on some future act of vengeance. Second, in this new trial of arms,
which the French both anticipated and feared, France could not
expect to triumph without the allied support which had permitted the
victory of 1918. Indeed, the very most that she could hope for on her
own was to thwart German attempts at a quick victory and so to effect
a prolonged military stalemate in the west. Then, having secured this
'draw', and having launched her own national mobilisation effort —
industrial as well as military — France could await the tie-breaking contributions of her allies before undertaking the great strategic offensive
upon which all hopes of victory were pinned.

I intend to say little about the first of these assumptions. French
suspicions of Germany, though they wavered slightly in the mid-1920s
and from one circle of Frenchmen to another, remained more or less
constant throughout the period. Whether such suspicions were justified,
as the Nazi experience might suggest to some, or whether they assumed
the form of a self-fulfilling prophecy, as the same experience might
suggest to others, really is a matter for conjecture. Or at least for a
more careful analysis than space would permit us here. The second
assumption, however, requires more investigation, partly because it is
so central to the theme of a long war and partly because it is too often
overlooked in our appreciation of French policy in the 1930s.

As the French saw it, the odds against an unassisted victory over
Germany were insuperable. Demographically, the number of French
citizens was a third less than that of Germany, an alarming disparity in
an age which had just learned to count army divisions by the hundred
and armed combatants by the million. This demographic advantage not
only gave Germany the opportunity of fielding more fighting units but
also assured her of a greater industrial workforce upon which her armies
could depend for provisions. Materially, too, France faced deficiencies
which promised to be critical in the event of a new war, especially since
the accelerating pace of technology seemed to militate against the
stockpiling of actual weaponry much in advance of war. Virtually all of
her oil (99 per cent) and rubber (100 per cent) had to be imported
from overseas, imports upon which her automotive industry was
heavily dependent. Her iron and steel industries were similarly
dependent on imported coal (30 per cent), coke (71 per cent), nickel
(100 per cent), and manganese (100 per cent). So too did her electrical
industry rely on imports of copper (100 per cent), her munitions

industry on imported cotton (100 per cent) and lead metal (87 per cent), her chemical industry on foreign sources of sulphur and pyrites (80 per cent), and her shipbuilding and aircraft industries on all of these in their turn.[3]

Industrially, the problems were further complicated, for where Nature had deposited her richest mineral holdings — in the north-east and in the recovered Alsace-Lorraine — she also had left two natural highways for an invader from east of the Rhine. Here, for instance, lay the greatest concentration of metallurgical industry in France — 90 per cent of her iron ore, pig iron and steel production — a few hours by land and a few minutes by air from Germany's western land and air bases.[4] And where Nature herself had declined to dictate industrial location, French industry had done so on its own — displaying a particular preference for the Paris area, the seat of over 60 per cent of the aircraft industry and over 30 per cent of French oil storage reservoirs.[5]

For these reasons, therefore, successive French governments reckoned that France would be acutely vulnerable in the event of a new war with Germany — a conclusion which makes as much sense and which certainly is based on as persuasive a reasoning as that which detects in French anxiety the telltale signs of some deep-seated national malaise.

But if by these remarks on France's circumstances we have urged restraint on those who decry the absence of energetic — not to say aggressive — French measures against Germany in the 1930s, we have hardly deprived them of their case. It is true that Germany, too, faced comparable deficiencies. For instance, what she had in coal resources, particularly after reclaiming the Saar fields in 1935, she lacked in iron ore. By the same token, she was also heavily dependent on imports of natural rubber, crude oil, bauxite, copper and nickel ores. And it would only be fair to point out that if the Germans were within easy striking distance of the great industrial complex around Lille, the French were no further removed from the industrially rich Ruhr basin. What is more, in recent years we have been persuaded that those very limitations, this same awareness of economic vulnerability, contributed much to the kind of mobile armoured-air warfare which was articulated in the strategical and tactical notion of *blitzkrieg*.[6] From this, therefore, could it not be argued that French economic limitations need not have been critical, need not have been restrictive, had the French like the Germans chosen *blitzkrieg* over *sitzkrieg*? In the light of 1940, of course, such a question has assumed almost rhetorical proportions.

The point is, however, that we are not addressing the collapse of

1940 but rather what happened before it. And all that was clear in the 1930s was that both countries were moving in quite different directions so far as their respective grand strategies were concerned. And for equally valid reasons. Without the judgement of 1940, is it genuinely possible to brand the French as foolish for having put everything on a long war, and not the Germans for having put everything on a short war? The fact is that both sides were gambling, the French nervously aware that the idea of a long war would be totally discredited should the Germans secure an early victory, the Germans equally aware that time was on the side of any new Anglo-French coalition whose combined resources promised to be overwhelming.[7] In the wake of these considerations, therefore, it seems to me that we can pursue our enquiry with a clear conscience, for we are neither trying to make the French unique in the problems they faced, nor are we trying to insist that their solutions to those problems should have been identical to those chosen by the future victors of 1940.

One final word of introduction. Since this paper has been conceived in deliberately general terms, as reflections on a subject which has engaged my attention for some time, I will refer to the French general staff in similar fashion. The expression is used here with reference to the army alone, and without distinction between the *état-major général de l'armée,* the subsequent but co-existing *etat-major général de la défense nationale,* the supreme peacetime position afforded to the vice-president of the *Conseil Supérieur de la Guerre,* and the almost equally prestigious position of *Inspecteur-Général de l'Armée.* In the period 1935-1939, on which this chapter is mainly focused, the last two offices were held jointly by General Maurice Gamelin; in addition to which he also occupied the post of either chief of the army staff or, subsequently, chief of the national defence staff.

Although his predecessor, the sharp-tongued and mercurial Maxime Weygand, had been denied such an accumulation of prestige and responsibility, the phlegmatic Gamelin was held to be no meddler in affairs of state and therefore a safe candidate for multiple military office. From his headquarters in the Rue Saint Dominique and later the dingy fortress at Vincennes, Gamelin worked in relative harmony with a succession of war ministers — Fabry, Maurin, Daladier — towards the readying of France for war. It is then mainly Gamelin of whom we think, of his military cabinet under the loyal Colonel Petibon, of his principal collaborators, Generals Georges and Colson, when we employ this rather ill-defined expression, general staff.[8] In itself it is a generalisation, one which risks exaggerating the degree of unanimity and single-

mindedness that may have obtained within army headquarters. For the
purpose of these reflections, however, the advantages of such a generalisation outweigh its disadvantages.

Turning first to the question of French military strategy, it may be
well to begin by denying that it was 'defensive'. Lest by this one is
understood to mean that it was in fact 'offensive', we might just as well
deny that too. It was neither one nor the other. It was both. Never did
the French renounce the belief that the enemy would have to be
destroyed and the war won by means of an overpowering offensive.
Never did they forget one of the first lessons they had drawn from
1914, namely that the very first priority was to ensure the territorial
inviolability of France. Thus theirs was that of 'la stratégie défensive-
offensive'; in other words, of a two-stage war.[9] Only after the first stage
had been traversed, after all the defensive requirements had been satisfied and the offensive means fully assembled, would the time have come
for the commencement of the strategic offensive. That this first stage
might last as long as two years was deemed of no particular concern to
generals who anticipated a long war and in whose eyes the demands
for foolproof defensive and offensive measures alike merely underlined
the importance of long and laborious preparation.[10] Temporally, for
reasons which can only be explained with reference to our subsequent
remarks on diplomacy and the role of Britain, the French believed
themselves to be advantaged *vis-à-vis* the Germans.

Yet this belief in the victorious potential of a long war was constantly imperilled by the logical if disturbing conclusion that had to be
drawn about the dangers of a short war, one likely as not begun by a
sudden German *attaque brusquee*.[11] Temporally speaking, again, the
promise for France lay in her ability to survive the first two years of
war, the peril, conversely, in her failure to do so. Understandably, therefore, her peacetime preparations in the 1930s were devoted in very
large part to her defensive needs. And it was in this context that there
arose two of the key doctrinal concepts of the French general staff
between the wars. The first was the concept of the *front continu*, one
which spoke of the desire to prepare in advance of hostilities a very
long and powerful defensive line — long enough to inhibit outflanking
manoeuvres, powerful enough to deny frontal penetration.[12] In practical terms, those conceived in the late 1920s and implemented in the
early 1930s, this line would embrace the light Rhenish fortifications
south and west of Strasbourg, the more famous Maginot defences
between Lauterbourg and Longuyon, and then the hoped-for Belgian
line of defence along the Meuse to Liège and beyond. Here, in brief, was

France's continuous front, hinged in the middle by the wooded Ardennes, a front that was deliberately and explicitly designed to tempt history into a repeat performance. The Germans, it was assumed, would have no recourse but to replay their 1914 drive into Belgium, that small kingdom which the French now hoped to transform into a new Verdun.[13]

But the continuous front is in itself little more than an abstraction. What gave it meaning, military substance, was the concept of fire power, *la puissance du feu*. Whatever the depth of barbed wire and anti-tank obstacles that lay in advance of the major fortified regions around Metz and Lauter, whatever the concrete tonnage and techno-logical finesse which helped build the legend of the Maginot Line, it was to the guns that the French always turned, the fire power that would either keep the enemy at bay or decimate those bold or foolish enough to approach. And, in particular, it was to the artillery that the French looked, the heavy and generally immobile guns that had transformed so much of northern France into a lunar landscape a decade earlier and thus had testified to the awesome, destructive power of heavy shells. This was fire power as the French knew it, the kind of weaponry that had caused entire forests to vanish, and against which they were pre-paring themselves with reinforced concrete bunkers and specially trained underground garrisons known as the *écrivisses de rempart*. Here, behind and under the protective folds of the continuous front, these men were to sit, waging war at a distance, aiming their artillery pieces and their anti-tank guns in the direction of an enemy they assumed would go elsewhere.

In the north, north of the Meuse, there was to be another kind of war, still defensive at the outset but far more mobile in character. Indeed, the Maginot Line across the Palatinate, and the continuous front of which that Line was only one part, was designed to permit and not pre-empt the use of mobile forces elsewhere. Just as this front was intended to steer the German offensive towards Belgium, so the inten-tion also was to have a mobile force ready in the north for a quick and immediate French thrust into Belgium.[14] This was not, let it be said, a departure from the initially defensive definition of the war. Rather it was an essential part of it, for the idea was to direct those mobile French forces to the Belgian Meuse whereupon they would employ their motorised and mechanised units in accordance with the Belgian defence effort. Having been directed towards Belgium by virtue of the French defences further south, the Germans were thus to be thwarted in the north by Belgian fortifications reinforced by mobile French fire power.

Having averted both invasion and defeat in this manner, the French
then anticipated a protracted defensive campaign, during which the
Germans would obligingly weaken themselves through costly but futile
offensive charges while France prepared herself for the final settling of
accounts. Here it is that one needs raise yet another concept of French
war doctrine and strategic planning. Having used the continuous front
and superior fire power to halt the enemy where they wished to halt
him, the French then would turn their attention to the build-up of a
massive superiority in war *matériel*, on completion of which the
strategic offensive could begin. This concept of *matériel*, while clearly
party to the first stage of the war, was absolutely central to the second.
Briefly put, the idea was to mobilise the military and industrial resources
of France and her empire behind the now firmly entrenched defensive
front. It would be a long process of intensive national preparation;
indeed, this is precisely why it was reckoned that the defensive stage
might last as long as two years. Then, having shut off the enemy's own
offensive alternatives and so having sapped his morale, the French
offensive could begin, slowly and methodically, assured of an overwhelming superiority — three times more infantry, six times more
artillery, twelve times more munitions.[15]

As we know, things did not work out this way in 1940, for reasons
which exceed the scope of these reflections. All that can be done here,
all that need be done, is to explain in general terms the outline of
French land strategy in the 1930s and, perhaps, to suggest that this
strategy was far more coherent, more reasoned, than is often con-
tended. This is not to say that it was flawless. Certainly there lay in the
continuous front at least three potential weaknesses, each of which was
broadly familiar to the general staff. First, it presupposed that the
natural defences of the Ardennes 'buckle' were comparable to the
holding power of the artificially constructed fortifications to the south
and the north. Second, it presented the ticklish problem of requiring a
combination of both fixed and mobile forces — in the face of a political forum which had invested so much public money in the former
that the army's additional demands for the latter were sometimes seen
as being inconsistent, sometimes as merely excessive. Third, it placed a
heavy premium on Belgian co-operation, a fact which automatically
invoked the contribution which politicians and diplomats were expected to make to national defence planning.

Before turning to the subject of diplomacy, it should be emphasised
that this strategy, with its vision of a long, two-stage war, was not the

work of the service commanders alone. This was a comprehensive
national strategy and as such it was conceived, articulated and endorsed
by the civilian as well as the military command. The country's international role as an anti-revisionist power after 1919, the national determination to counter any new invasion attempt with a minimal toll in
precious French lives, the recognition of France's industrial and demographic inferiority to Germany, all served to induce general agreement
between military and civilian spokesmen. Having agreed on the necessity
of preparing for a long war, they thus collaborated within such bodies
as the *Conseil Supérieur de la Defénse Nationale,* the *Haut Comité
Militaire,* the *Comité Permanent de la Defense Nationale* and the parliamentary service commissions to realise the defensive installations
required by the continuous front and, less certainly, to constitute the
motorised and mechanised units of the mobile defence arm.[16] The idea
of *matériel* also provided common ground for soldier and civilian,
although it is true that this critical concept did evoke certain differences in emphasis. For instance, feelings sometimes ran high between
civilians who were preoccupied with long-range economic planning for
war and soldiers who were intent on beefing up their actual combat
forces.[17] Nevertheless, however much the generals might press their case
for augmenting the fire power of the standing divisions, their memories
of the First World War now cautioned them against begrudging rival
expenditures on new serial production facilities, or raw material stockpiles, or oil surplus reservoirs.[18]

In all these areas, and many more besides, successive French governments in the 1930s were a good deal more active than is generally
acknowledged — and not in spite of the national security question but
precisely because of it.[19] While it is true that the forums for frequent
and formal exchanges between soldiers and civilians were poorly
developed in France, offering nothing that was really comparable to the
Committee of Imperial Defence in Britain, at the highest level of
strategic planning it must be said that there was a broad consensus
between the civilian and military authorities.

Within the ranks of this civilian command there was a special group
of public servants, distinct from the cabinet ministers who oversaw all
planning, the secretariat which served the war ministry, the legions of
civil servants who arranged such matters as oil purchases, aircraft con-
tracts and industrial relocation settlements. This was the diplomatic
corps. With its headquarters on the Quai d'Orsay, the French foreign
ministry was to assume a central role in the realisation of the national
strategy. Indeed, it is only with reference to this strategy that one could

justify treating the foreign ministers of this period as men of like per-
suasion — such disparate types as Louis Barthou and Georges Bonnet,
Pierre Laval and Yvon Delbos, Pierre Etienne Flandin and Joseph Paul-
Boncour. Similarly, to treat as an homogeneous, like-minded group
such ambassadors as Francois-Poncet, Coulondre, Laroche, Noel, Puaux
and Corbin, or such ministerial directors as Léger, Massigli, Bargeton,
Charvériat and Comert, is to spin a concentric web without purpose or
validity unless it is fashioned around the central beam of the national
strategy. And again, it is only with reference to this strategy, and to
the vision of a long war from which that strategy derived, that one can
hope to explain the course and objectives of French foreign policy in
the 1930s. Conversely, it is only with reference to this policy that we
can hope to understand the *raison d'être* of that same grand strategy.

In short, the picture we have to this point is still very incomplete.
Indeed, a moment's reflection on our remarks so far would suggest that
something was much amiss. Our references to the industrial and demographic gap would go far to explain French doubts about defeating
Germany singlehandedly, their persistent fear of surprise German
attack. They would do little to explain, however, and much to contra-
dict, the idea of defeating Germany in a long war. If they feared being
overrun in a short campaign, how could they imagine defeating their
industrially superior neighbour in a long war? It makes little sense,
indeed no sense at all, unless one is to invoke the vital importance
which the French attributed to allied assistance. But for allies, the
French believed, their chances of warding off a German invasion were
doubtful in the extreme, their chances of defeating Germany virtually
negligible.

So enter the diplomats, the men whose first task it was to prevent
the war from which France had little to gain, but whose second responsibility was to prepare the ground for a powerful wartime alliance — the
kind of coalition that had helped avert defeat in 1914 and had helped
secure victory in 1918. For this purpose, and speaking very generally,
the French had three kinds of combination in mind. First, they
intended to make all that they could of the 1920 alliance with Belgium.
After all, their entire war plan rested on the idea of confronting the
German invader on the Belgian Meuse. Second, they intended to fashion
a second front in eastern Europe, with or without the assistance of the
Soviet Union. This front, centred on Czechoslovakia and rounded out
by Poland to the north and Romania and Yugoslavia to the south, was
expected to pin down and harass the forces which Germany would be
obliged to retain in the east, a role to which the French themselves

might contribute should it prove possible to establish a new bridgehead at Salonika.[20] Third, there was Britain, the *pierre de touche* for all French strategic planning between the wars.

So much has been written about French dependence on Britain in this period, French deference, French subservience, that one is not expected to pass up the parasitic inference. Besides, it sits so well with the apparent weakness of France in 1940 that it would almost affront our sense of historical continuity to suggest otherwise. Yet affronted this sense should be, if in carefully measured terms. How very tempting it would be, just for once, to insist that it was really the French who dictated British foreign policy in the 1930s. Tempting but, one must confess, quite untenable. Rather, the historian of France between the wars simply has to accept that the French sense of dependence on Britain has not been exaggerated. But it has been very badly understood, for that sense of dependence did not stem from a country that was too tired, too indifferent, to resist the German peril. In fact, it derived from a set of very practical and concrete circumstances which the French took, and perhaps quite rightly took, to be pivotal to any successful resistance of German revanchism.

Wherever the French looked, and it might be argued wherever the British looked as well, they detected an Anglo-French community of interest. Neither had the slightest reason to welcome a German presence in the Lowlands; neither could accept any threat to its vital Mediterranean supply routes – whether it be from Italy, Spain, Germany or any combination thereof;[21] and neither desired major changes in the postwar territorial *status quo* in the Near or Far East. Moreover, for their part the French recognised that Britain was an essential prerequisite for the prosecution of the only kind of war that France actually could hope to win against Germany.[22] Quite apart from their intention of securing an actual military commitment to the continent, the French were determined to assure British support in other ways as well. In wartime, for instance, they knew that almost a third of their vital coal supplies would have to be imported from the British Isles, just as they acknowledged their heavy dependence on a British merchant fleet whose ships normally carried a third (32 per cent) of France's commercial tonnage. Similarly, they appreciated the fact that over a third (35 per cent) of all their trade by value derived from Britain and her empire, and that this same source provided the lion's share of French imports of jute, rubber, tin, wool and manganese. Finally, since over half (55 per cent) of all French seaborne imports were received in the Channel ports, they were also aware of their dependence on the disposition of the Royal Navy.[23]

Furthermore, and very much along the lines that the British themselves
were pursuing, the French believed that the successful negotiation of
stage one of the war would depend on the offensive arm of the combined Anglo-French naval forces.

In short, not only was Germany to be bottled up in Belgium while
France churned out the requisite *matériel* for the offensive stage of the
war, but in the interval Germany was to be reduced to a stage of siege
by a rigorous, joint naval blockade. It was this naval supremacy that
would ensure France free access to her own vital imports and that
conversely would separate Germany from hers. Britain, still the chief
naval power in European waters, was therefore not only an obvious but
indeed the indispensable ally in French strategic calculations. As one
war ministry memorandum declared, 'nous ne pourrions sortir vain-
queurs d'une guerre avec l'Allemagne que si nous etait acquise, dans
tous les domaines, l'aide totale de la Grande Bretagne.'[24] Little wonder,
therefore, that the French should strive with such determination to
recapture that so-long elusive alliance with England. And once again,
not because they had lost the will to resist, but because they had kept
it alive.

Such were the chief objectives of French diplomacy in the 1930s,
objectives which for a time at least were entirely consistent with the
higher goals of strategic planning. But as often happens, theory came to
clash rudely and unhappily with circumstance. Take the case of
Belgium. The Belgian problem has been judged by some as inherently
'insoluble', one of those rare occasions when what might have been
appears to have been the same as what actually was.[25] Though the
writing had long been on the wall, the Belgians at last decided to scrap
their alliance with France in the course of 1936, for a variety of domestic and international reasons. Although subsequent arrangements were
contrived in order to keep alive the possibility of a future Franco-
Belgian defence effort, the French had to admit that their continuous
front now appeared much abbreviated — an admission that soon spurred
them to a new fortification effort along their frontier with Belgium.[26]

The eastern front idea proved equally disappointing. In the first
place, it was never to materialise into a real front, conceived as it had
been only by a series of bilateral agreements — of varying intimacy —
between France and each of the interested powers.[27] In particular, the
Poles and Czechs refused to see eye to eye; the Romanians and
Yugoslavs were more concerned about Italy and Hungary than they
were with Germany; and most of these competing French allies were
troubled by the French decision to conclude a mutual assistance

pact with Russia in 1935. Thus it was difficult indeed for the French to forge a united coalition when their eastern partners could identify neither common enemies nor, apart from France herself, common friends.

In the second place, the attempts to shape such a coalition ultimately gave rise to a troublesome dilemma for French strategists. While in theory the eastern front was entirely compatible with French strategy, its implementation called for measures that the French were reluctant to undertake. For instance, commitments to the defence of France could only be secured by means of reciprocal French commitments to the defence of the prospective ally. So long as France became the initial victim of German aggression, as the French long anticipated would be the case, the allied pledges to French security were wholly in keeping with French strategic planning. If, however, those other powers should be the first to fall victim to German attack – a possibility that grew after 1933 with the Nazi doctrine of *lebensraum* – the situation would be reversed. France's alliances might now entangle her in conflicts that were far removed from her own borders and her own immediate security. In this sense, therefore, French diplomacy promised to increase, rather than diminish, the likelihood of a new war.

No less disturbing, for the French as well as for their eastern clients, was the demand imposed by the eastern front for a much accelerated French offensive effort. Unless the French were prepared to launch early and serious offensive operations in the west, on behalf of their threatened eastern allies, the credibility of their search for a powerful alliance system was bound to suffer. Yet to have done so, to have prepared for such a contingency, would have risked compromising yet another part of that strategy – that which was predicated on an opening defensive stage and on the attendant injunction against early and reckless offensives.[28]

It was this internal tension within the national strategy that was to come to the fore most clearly at the time of Munich, when the general staff refused to recommend energetic military measures on behalf of an ally whom they regarded as central to their strategic calculations. As the premier of the day later concluded, the generals had given all their attention to an awesome 'guerre de coalition' and none to the possibility of a France 'qui serait seule à secourir la Tchécoslovaquie'.[29]

The strategic dilemma which was evoked by the eastern front idea was further compounded by the ambivalence with which this idea was received in London. If earlier British concerns about French continental hegemony had been allayed by the 1930s, they had been replaced by ones grounded in the fear of seeing France overextended in the east. In other words, and very much as many French observers also feared, French alliance diplomacy seemed to have increased the chances of a new confrontation with Germany. This, the British disliked on principle, and all the more so whenever the French urged upon them the speedy conclusion of a formal Anglo-French alliance. Since Britain herself had been loath to accept direct commitments to the security of eastern Europe, it was understandable that she should be reluctant to assume them indirectly by virtue of an alliance with France. In this sense, then, France's pursuit of alliances in the east complicated and impeded her pursuit of the vital alliance with Britain. On the other hand, it may be argued that this same French presence in the east also contributed to the British interest in preserving the unwritten, informal entente with France. The fact was, as one astute professional in the Foreign Office later conceded, that presence had enabled Britain to exercise an influence in an area of Europe to which she remained formally uncommitted until 1939.[30] By holding out the promise of a true alliance with France, while withholding the substance, the British were able to insinuate themselves into the shaping of French policy in the 1930s and by so doing to press moderation and restraint on the directors of the Quai d'Orsay.

Realising full well that such intervention was really designed to avoid British involvement on the continent, the French had no choice but to accept this shrewd, frequent and often effective meddling. Again, their vision of a long war, and the grand strategy which they had devised to accord with that vision, left them with little alternative. All that they could do was await that moment when British attempts to evade continental commitments had succeeded in accomplishing the exact reverse. It was this that Chamberlain unwittingly secured at Munich, for by the contribution he made to the weakening of France through the loss of Czechoslovakia, he rendered unavoidable an increased British commitment to France.

The irony was that it seemed to have taken this blow to French prestige and influence before the British could admit, in ambassador Corbin's words, that 'l'alliance francaise présente aux yeux de l'Angleterre une véritable pierre de touche'.[31] From this came, in the succeeding months, the very alliance which the French had coveted and which Chamberlain himself had sought to avoid. Until that happened, however, the French were obliged to play their hand with infinite tact, tolerating British meddling, deferring to British pressure whenever there was a genuine difference of opinion between them. But by so doing, by pur-

suing with such consistency and perseverance the one indispensable ally
in their strategic calculations, they inevitably gave rise to the impression
that they had lost the will to resist, that they had succumbed to a policy
of aimless drift and dithering.

That impression, of course, has drawn much of its force from the
more famous diplomatic crises of the 1930s, crises which too often
have been nimbly threaded together in order to demonstrate the
forfeiture of French diplomatic independence. Although this should be
acclaimed as a feat of quite remarkable dexterity, the trick behind this
sleight of hand is fairly readily exposed. It consists of convincing an
audience that French policy was really British, that the French invari-
ably took their counsels in London, and therefore that they repeatedly
bowed to the British government: in 1935 over the Ethiopian crises, in
1936 over the Rhineland and Spanish crises, in 1938 over the Austrian
and Czech crises. But however much one admires such crafted symme-
try, in this case it is the work of magicians.

Of the five crises to which we have referred, two were not crises at
all, at least not for the French. They had no intention of fighting for
either the Rhineland or for Austria, and therefore were hardly in need
of British appeals for restraint. The 'crises' were allowed to surface only
after the matter had been effectively settled, post facto, and contrived
French legends designed to hoodwink us into thinking that France
might have resisted had it not been for the calming hand of the English.
Nor is the evidence associated with the Spanish crisis persuasive enough
to convince us that France's policy of non-intervention was really
hammered out in Whitehall. Here, or so it seems to me, was yet another
French policy, proposed in accordance with French domestic circumstances and only secondarily with Britain's clearly stated preference for
non-involvement. Unlike the preceding three, however, the Ethiopian
and Czech crises did reflect major and genuine differences of opinion
between the British and French governments — in the case of the
former because the British appeared from Paris to be too reckless in
courting hostilities with Italy, in the case of the latter because they
appeared too timid about risking war with Germany. In both cases the
French did resolve on policies that they would not have pursued in the
absence of strong and persistent British pressure.

The point to be drawn from such crises, however, is not that such
deference to Britain either proved or disproved some iron rule, but rather
that there had never been such a rule in the first place. However much
the French themselves often sought to conceal the fact, there was
always a French policy, conceived and pursued for indigenous French

reasons. On those occasions when that policy happened to accord with British thinking, the French simply carried on apace. On those occasions when it did not, when France's preferred policy promised to exacerbate relations with England, they reshaped that policy to accord with the wishes of the one ally to whom their own strategic appreciations had awarded pride of place.[32]

The same call for discretion should be heeded when it comes to assessing the role of the general staff in French foreign policy, for it would be as much of an exaggeration to see that policy as one designed by the generals as it would be to portray it as one designed by the British. In very broad terms I have sought to emphasise the connection between French diplomacy and French strategic assumptions. While such an emphasis is certainly not intended to deny considerations of say an economic or an ideological nature, it has been deliberately and specifically directed at the role which allies were to assume in French grand strategy.

This role, of course, was of the greatest interest to the French general staff whose officers usually applauded any diplomatic effort that was likely to preserve — though not necessarily enlarge upon — the existing alliance network. Thus they supported the cultivation of the alliances with Belgium, Poland and Czechoslovakia, and the far less binding ties with Romania and Yugoslavia. Similarly, they welcomed the 1935 pact with Russia, just as they approved of the government's decision to deny the Soviets a military convention; and certainly they remained partisans of a closer agreement with Italy, even after the Ethiopian crisis and the advent of the Popular Front government in France had taken the probability out of such a development. For them, as for the diplomats whose attitudes on such matters broadly corresponded with those of the generals, the strategic importance of the allies was quite undeniable. In short, the requirements of the national strategy were so clear, so universally accepted, that the officers and the diplomats were generally agreed on what had to be done. At this very basic level, strategy, like war itself, was no more the preserve of the soldiers than it was of the civilian leadership.

Regrettably perhaps, the role of the general staff in the specific crisis situations is similarly unspectacular. Granted, it can be argued that on each of these occasions the generals did nothing to discourage, and indeed tacitly approved, the policies of inaction upon which successive cabinets seemed to settle. And from this one might be tempted to conclude that these policies were somehow, in some way, inspired by the generals themselves. But negative arguments like this will not carry us very far, particularly if they be marshalled with one eye on a pattern that once again is more apparent than real.

At the height of the Ethiopian crisis there was not one appeal from the military advisers, there were two. Do not forfeit the burgeoning alliance with Italy; do nothing to jeopardise the prospects of securing an alliance with England. This, as we all know, was at the heart of Laval's dilemma as premier; and the general staff had no greater professional advice to offer in resolving this dilemma than to urge him to hold fast to the disintegrating Stresa front. Thus while it is true that they repeatedly underscored the strategic importance of both Italy and Britain, and while that issue was absolutely central to French perceptions of that crisis, it would be more accurate to say that the soldiers agreed with rather than actively pressed for the government's reluctant decision to side with Britain and the League.

Then there was the Rhineland affair of March 1936, in the course of which certain cabinet ministers sought to attribute French inaction to discouraging military advice.[33] Though it is clear that these professional assessments were pitched unmistakably to the side of caution, and this despite the realisation that the loss of the Rhineland would sever France from eastern Europe,[34] two other points are equally apparent. First, the politicians had done next to nothing to see that a military contingency plan had been prepared in advance of this long-awaited German coup; second, what they were told in March 1936 about the French army's unreadiness for immediate offensive action was about as novel as frost in a prairie winter. The fact was that the Rhenish demilitarised zone was never regarded as a sufficient cause for war with Germany, a fact that was publicly inadmissible in 1936 and which therefore provoked a scramble among soldiers and civilians to find some pretext for failing to take energetic measures.[35]

The Spanish and Austrian crises similarly provided little opportunity for an active, interventionist military voice. Indeed, so far as we can tell, the army staff was never even consulted by Premier Blum over the nonintervention decision, just as no evidence has yet come to light that would suggest that the army was ever seriously requested to contemplate active measures on behalf of a threatened Austria.[36]

The Czech crisis, it seems to me, was quite different in this respect. This time the general staff was asked repeatedly for its views on the chances of preventing the destruction of Czechoslovakia — an indication, one might venture, of Premier Daladier's own inclination to call what he regarded as Hitler's bluff. As I have argued in much greater detail elsewhere,[37] the general staff refused to make a case for war on behalf of the Czechs, and for reasons which I have alluded to earlier in this paper. What is more, this time, precisely because the possibility of accepting the risk of war was given serious consideration, the views of the soldiers may well have been more influential than is often acknowledged.

This military advice, especially that which we encounter in the autumn of 1938, did not have to be particularly explicit. This was just as well, for the French peacetime commander-in-chief was Maurice Gamelin, a ventriloquist of a general who could speak volumes without moving his lips. Unlike his outspoken predecessor, Maxime Weygand, Gamelin was a consummate practitioner of military *mutisme*, one of the few professional subjects about which he had much to say. For him the general staff officer was a technician, one who advised the government on request but only in terms which neither compromised political sovereignty nor invited upon the army the dreaded responsibility for misguided policies. The problem, however, was that Gamelin also recognised folly when he saw it coming, or at least thought he did; and this prescience was sometimes allowed to play havoc with his scruples about military obedience. So it was that this supreme officer not infrequently turned his very considerable talents to the art of the *double entendre*, confidently predicting that Czechoslovakia could be resurrected from defeat — after a long and terrible war, blithely assuring Daladier that France would remain master of the situation — so long as she avoided the outbreak of hostilities, boldly declaring that the army was 'ready' — for mobilisation, if not for war.[38]

The fact was, however, that this ever *triste* military advice never needed to be very direct or explicit. For beneath the specifics of each famous crisis lay the bedrock of French grand strategy, a strategy that assumed a joint Anglo-French effort in a war of long duration. Owing to these ever-intrusive strategic calculations a war with Germany simply could not be risked without assurances of active British support; and therefore this war would not be countenanced until the British government had fully awakened to the peril of German continental hegemony. Indeed, by some strange and terrible irony it seemed necessary for France to endure a progressive weakening of her own continental situation before the British would come alive to her importance as an ally, before they would acknowledge the vital contribution which she was expected to make to their own plans for conducting a long and protracted war.

Thereafter, after the shock waves of Munich slowly began altering the diplomatic landscape, it was really more the role than the influence of the general staff that increased. After all, once the British had agreed in February 1939 to the early initiation of serious joint staff talks, the single most important request that French generals had ever made to their diplomats was on the point of being realised. In this sense, then, what Gamelin and his staff had to say about specific diplomatic problems was of even less moment than ever. They were not asked to do anything about the German takeover of Prague in March 1939, only to join in a collective sigh of relief over the elimination of the one loose end left over from Munich. They had even less to say than the Quai d'Orsay itself about Chamberlain's announced joint guarantee to Poland at the end of that same month. And their general reluctance to invite hostilities with Italy was indistinguishable from the Anglo-French political inclination to minimise tensions in the Mediterranean and North Africa in the early stages of the war. They were finally asked, of course, to take charge of the negotiations with Russia in August 1939, in response to the Soviet insistence that a military convention precede any political accord. But here one has the impression that the general staff in Paris neglected its own military delegation, leaving mission members like General Doumenc and Captain Beaufre to argue unsuccessfully with the likes of General Musse — the war ministry's own military attaché in Warsaw.[39] And for all the controversy which has sprung up around the famous meeting of 23 August 1939 — when the Daladier government rather informally decided to fight for Poland in the event of German aggression — that decision was effectively taken *before* the specific military appreciations had been tendered by the French chiefs of staff. The latter clearly did not have to sell the idea of standing with Britain and Poland. On the contrary, they would have been very hard pressed to discredit it.

Nevertheless, if not the influence certainly the role of the general staff expanded significantly in the spring of 1939. It was now up to the military technicians to turn an at last promising diplomatic arrangement into a practical military contract, the contract that both sides now believed was essential to the prosecution of the anticipated long war with the Axis powers. To this end, while civilians from both sides of the Channel worked on such questions as oil, coal and food supplies, the military delegations laboured over matters like those of the British Expeditionary Force, the British Advanced Air Striking Force, the deployment of their naval forces around the globe, and the joint utilisation of the radar and asdic detection systems.[40] Throughout the summer of 1939, therefore, the French army staff worked with its air and naval counterparts to realise the English alliance in concrete military terms — an alliance which their diplomats, with Hitler's help, had finally secured, an alliance which those same diplomats had pursued from the start in the broader interests of French grand strategy.

It is for these reasons that the idea of a long war suggests itself as a useful vehicle for adding to our understanding of French foreign policy and French military policy in the 1930s. This idea, rooted securely but not frivolously in the experiences of the First World War, served as the driving force behind French military strategy. Yet that strategy, in its turn, imposed great and challenging demands on French diplomats. A failure to see that connection must inhibit our grasp and understanding of both endeavours, the diplomatic and the military. Especially central to French diplomacy is the pivotal role which the military and civilian strategists had awarded to Britain. This paper has tried, on the one hand, to explain French attachment to the idea of a British alliance, without having recourse to the vocabulary of malaise, drift and defeatism. On the other hand, it has warned against seeing in every French policy, every moment of apparent, and sometimes fabricated, crisis, the thinly veiled countenance of an English 'gouvernante'.[41] Similarly, while we have argued against seeing in each of these crises the active hand of the general staff, we have also suggested that the chief of staff did advise the government more often than he cared to admit and sometimes, as in the Czech crisis, with very considerable effect.

But again, on such occasions as these, that which was of the greatest importance was less the specific appreciations of the moment and more the underlying recognition that the long war for which France had prepared was unthinkable without an assured alliance with Great Britain. La guerre de longue durée had long since ceased to be merely an expression. It had become a state of mind, according to the lights of which French soldiers and diplomats worked uneasily towards the cataclysm which they had sense enough to fear. And for them, we are obliged to remember, it was indeed something to fear. But it was a fear of the known, rather than of the unknown, fear of what they expected — a long, drawn-out war — rather than a fear of what they did not expect — sudden defeat. Given their vision of the war to come, is it so difficult to fathom why the French did not litter the streets with flowers in 1939 as they had done in 1914, why their response to war this time was more cerebral, less fanciful? Could it be that the partic- ular kind of war they anticipated had something to do with the calm but sober atmosphere that hung over the Gare de l'Est in September 1939, as men with ready memories of the last war prepared to depart for the front, not for adventure but for sacrifice?

Notes

1. D.C. Watt, *Too Serious a Business*, London, Temple Smith, 1975, p. 86.
2. At the same time we have also been warned against assuming the illogicality of the short war assumption – '. . . the younger Moltke's modification of Schlieffen's original conception . . . may well have been the factor which deprived Germany of an early and overwhelming triumph.' Cf. R.D. Challener, *The French Theory of the Nation In Arms, 1866-1939*, New York, Russell and Russell, 1965, p. 114.
3. Cf. 'General survey of national resources of France', 6 March 1939, *Public Record Office* (PRO) FO 371, 22916, C 2737/130/17; Economic Warfare Synopsis (France), July 1939, *PRO*, FO 837/1B; CSDN note, 'Le potentiel économique de la France', *Daladier Papers*, 2 DA4/Dr3/sdr a.
4. Ibid.
5. CPDN meeting, report of M. Ramadier, 9 October 1937, *Service Historique de l'Armée* (SHA); *Handbook of the French Air Forces*, appendix xviii, January 1939, *PRO*, Air 10.
6. See A. Milward, *The German Economy at War*, London, Athlone Press, 1965, 1-27; B.H. Klein, *Germany's Economic Preparations for War*, Cambridge, Harvard University Press, 1959, pp. 28-64.
7. For an examination of German concerns see B.A. Carroll's study of General Georg Thomas in *Design for Total War: Arms and Economics in the Third Reich*, The Hague, Mouton, 1968. Germany reportedly entered the war in 1939 with only a few months' supply of critical items like petrol, fuel, oil, rubber, copper and iron ore. See Klein, op. cit., pp. 4, 56-9.
8. Alphonse Georges, major-general of the armies and commander designate for the north-east theatre of operations; Louis Colson, chief of the army headquarters staff and principal executor of the army's rearmament section; Jean Petibon, long-serving member of Gamelin's personal staff, initially in charge of relations with foreign armies, ultimately named chief of Gamelin's *état-major* in 1939.
9. A. Krebs, 'Considerations sur l'Offensive', *Revue Militaire Générale*, September 1937, pp. 324-65.
10. Recalling his remarks of August 1939, Gamelin later testified: 'Mais je n'ai pas caché que nous ne pourrions obtenir de résultat contre l'Allemagne qu'au prix d'une guerre longue et que ce n'était qu'en 1941 ou 1942 que nous pourrions prendre l'offensive.' Riom deposition, 28 September 1940, *Daladier Papers*, 4 DA 24/Dr5/sdr a.
11. As Challener points out, the industrial dimension of modern war aggravated the fear of sudden attack, for an aggressor could timetable his own war production to mature at a fixed point in time – thus assuring himself of an early advantage over his intended victim. See Challener, op. cit., p. 189.
12. For a fuller treatment of this principle, see the author's 'Preparations for Defeat: French War Doctrine in the Inter-War Period', *Journal of European Studies*, ii, No. 2, June 1972, pp. 155-72.
13. As deputy chief of staff General Victor Schweisguth admitted in April 1936: 'En effet la fermeture réciproque par des fortifications de la frontière franco-allemand ne pourra avoir pour résultat que de rejeter des

opérations éventuelles vers des terrains plus ouverts, c'est-à-dire vers la Belgique et la Hollande.' *Schweisguth Papers,* Dr 12/ sdr a/ annex 4.

14. Central to this operation was the belief that Germany's armoured divisions would not be thrown against the well-prepared French defences to the south, but rather used for 'des actions rapides contre des adversaires relativement faibles et en terrain libre; c'est le cas de . . . la Belgique dont l'armée est trop faible pour saturer les espaces qu'elle doit tenir'. Gamelin to the *Conseil Supérieur de la Guerre* (CSG), 29 April 1936, *SHA.*

15. Such at least was the formula proposed by Marshal Pétain in his preface to General Chauvineau's *Une Invasion est-elle encore possible?*, Paris, Editions Berger-Levrault, 1939, p. vii.

16. For the organisation, composition and responsibilities of these various inter-ministerial planning committees, see J. Vial, 'La defénse nationale: son organisation entre les deux guerres', *Revue d'Histoire de la Deuxième Guerre Mondiale,* No. 18, April 1955, pp. 11-32.

17. The dilemma was particularly pronounced over the uses to which the enormous national gold reserve should be put — whether to deplete that reserve in the interests of remedying immediate needs or whether to hoard it in anticipation of colossal wartime expenditures.

18. Thus, while we find instances of generals bitterly resisting cuts in their standing forces, we also find them acknowledging the importance of long-range economic planning in general and of raw material stockpiling in particular. Cf. CSG meeting, 18 December 1933, *SHA,* and Daladier's Riom testimony, 3 March 1942, *Blum Papers,* 3BL/Dr 15; and HCM meeting, 9 February 1935, *SHA,* and Gamelin to Daladier, 21 March 1938, *Daladier Papers,* 4 DA3/Dr1/sdr a.

19. The famous *Loi sur l'organisation de la nation en temps de guerre* of 1938 is but one testament to this fact — an elaborate piece of legislation for the conduct of war in its broadest sense, a law which had been conceived a decade earlier and at least partly implemented, measure by measure, in the interval.

20. The Salonika idea, deriving from the Balkan campaigns of 1915-18, remained much alive in French army calculations throughout the 1930s. For instance, see entries of 20 November 1936 and 22 February 1937 in *Schweisguth Papers,* 351 AP3/Dr10/Dr11.

21. For instance, in the mid 1930s just over a third of all French seaborne imports and exports by weight were conveyed via the Mediterranean, with 20 per cent of the imports received in Mediterranean ports. More than 60 per cent of all French imports were seaborne. Cf. 'General survey . . . ', March 1939, *PRO,* FO 371, 22916, C2737/130/17.

22. This attitude was reinforced by the aggravating effects which the Depression had on the Franco-German industrial imbalance. Between 1929 and 1937, by French reckoning, their production had declined by 25 per cent compared to a 17 per cent increase in German production — the kind of increase that had allowed Germany to overtake France by 1937 in aircraft, automobile and naval construction. Cf. 'Du rôle du secrétariat-général du ministère de la défense nationale et de la guerre . . . ', and 'Note sur la mobilisation industrielle', 5 April 1939, *Daladier Papers,* 4 DA2/Dr2, and 4 DA4/Dr1.

23. See 'Notes on the principal industrial factors', August 1935, *PRO,* CAB 55/7 and 'General survey . . . ', March 1939, *PRO,* FO 371, 22916, C2737/130/17.

24. 'Note sur la mobilisation industrielle', 5 April 1939, *Daladier Papers,* 4 DA4/Dr1.

25. Henri Michel, *The Second World War*, London, Deutsch, 1975, 20.
26. Cf. General P.E. Tournoux, *Haut Commandement: Gouvernement et Défense des Frontières du Nord et l'Est, 1919-1939*, Paris, Nouvelles Editions Latines, 1960, pp. 260-71, 290-2.
27. See *League of Nations: Treaty Series*, Vols. xviii (1923), xxiii (1924), lviii (1926-7), lxviii (1927).
28. It was with reference to such injunctions that the French air force presented itself as the sole offensive arm capable of immediate action. As the air minister, Pierre Cot, insisted, a German attack in the east would find the French army 'sur la défensive et seules les Forces Aériennes pourraient agir'. *Haut Comité Militaire*, 20 March 1933, *SHA*. See also his letter to Blum, 27 July 1936, *Service Historique de l'Armée de l'Air* (SHAA), B 70.
29. 'Munich' by Edouard Daladier, *Daladier Papers*, 2 DA1/Dr5. One might add that his despair was all the greater as he realised that Germany's piecemeal conquest of eastern Europe could assure Hitler of the means he would need 'de mener la guerre de longue durée'.
30. '. . . to put it crudely we have used the French army and the French system of alliances as one of the instruments with which to exert our authority on the continent . . . used France as a shield, behind which we have maintained ourselves in Europe since our disarmament.' Minute by Orme Sargent, 17 October 1938, *PRO*, FO 371, 21612, C12162/1050/17.
31. Corbin to Bonnet, 8 November 1938, *Daladier Papers*, 2DA4/Dr/sdr a.
32. The details of this argument and the justification for the conclusions that are offered in the above text have been developed at some length in the author's recently completed book, 'In Command of France: French Foreign Policy and Military Planning in the Nazi Years, 1933-1940.' (To be published by Harvard University Press.)
33. Gamelin privately dismissed as 'intolérable' the criticism he drew from ministers like Flandin, Sarraut and Paul-Boncour. Nevertheless, he also privately admitted to the CSG that 'les militaires ont été obligés de freiner les hommes politiques'. See entries of 9 March and 22 April 1936, *Schweisguth Papers*, 351 AP3/ Dr8 (Rapports et Conferences).
34. Indeed, Gamelin had told the HCM in January 1935: 'si la zone disparait, si les Allemands construisent des fortifications, ils bousclent la France et sont capables d'être maîtres a l'Est.' HCM meeting, 23 January 1935, *SHA*.
35. While it is true that the French public responded to this 'crisis' with absolute calm, it was clear to all that France had been humiliated by the unilateral violation of the Locarno accord. Moreover, by keeping the 'crisis' alive, by pretending that war remained a possibility, the French government not only saved some face but also managed to extort a new British guarantee for French security in mid-March 1936.
36. Daladier, war minister in March 1938, later admitted: 'On ne pouvait agir qu'indirectement, en inquiétant Hitler, par le renforcement de nos effectifs aux frontières.' The 'plan' for such measures, however, was none other than that for partial mobilisation, the same one which surfaced every time any kind of military action was even remotely contemplated. Cf. Daladier's *notes manuscrites*, DA7/Dr6.
37. See the author's 'Le Haut Commandement Français au moment de Munich', *Revue d'Histoire Moderne et Contemporaine*, vol. xxiv (Janvier-Mars 1977), pp 110-29.
38. Cf. Gamelin to Daladier, 16 March 1938, attached to CPDN meeting of 15 March, 'Archives du Général Gamelin', *SHA* : Gamelin's record of a meeting with Daladier, 12 September 1938, in his *Servir*, pp. ii, 346-7; 'Note sur la Reúnion du 23 Août', 25 December 1940, *La Chambre Papers*. See also P. Le Goyet, *Le Mystère Gamelin*, Paris, Presses de la Cité, 1975.

39.   Cf. A. Beaufre, *Le drame de 1940*, Paris, Plon, 1965, pp. 155-60; General
       Musse to War Ministry, 18-20 August 1939, and Leon Noel to Bonnet, 19
       August 1939, *Daladier Papers*, 2DA6/Dr6/sdr b.
40.   Select references to this topic would include, *PRO*, CAB 29/159/160; Air
       9/104/105/116; ADM 116/3767, ADM I/9905, 9962, 9898; Dennis
       Richards, *RAF Narrative*, unpublished, Air Historical Branch; J. Brown,
       'Anglo-French Naval Conversations 1939', *Anglo-French Colloquium*,
       unpublished, 1973; Buckley, Neave-Hill, Haslam, 'Anglo-French Staff Con-
       versations, 1938-39', *Les Relations Franco-Britanniques 1935-39*, Paris,
       CNRS, 1975, pp. 91-118; P. Fridenson and J. Lecuir, *La France et la
       Grande Bretagne face aux problèmes aériens, 1935-mai 1940*, Vincennes,
       SHAA, 1976.
41.   F. Bedarida, 'La "Gouvernante Anglaise"', *Colloque Daladier*, unpublished,
       1975.

4 STALIN AND THE RED ARMY GENERAL STAFF IN THE THIRTIES

Albert Seaton

In chapter 2 we read of how the German General Staff, and in particular the Army High Command, abdicated their proper role to the German dictator, and how, in their pursuit of gain and fame — or through fear — many senior German generals deliberately closed their eyes to the significance of the events of the time.

In many respects the Russian story is the same, a fairly close parallel to the developments in Berlin. The Soviet terror was certainly no less than the Nazi; the *Waffen-SS* had its equivalent in the NKVD, the Gestapo and Sicherheitsdienst in the KGB.[1] The Red Army generals, no less than the Hitlerite ones, were mere cogs in the state machine and were often used as tools to destroy their fellows; they were certainly not the men to speak out against the injustices, the inhumanity and the atrocities that were going on around them. And of course much of the apparatus of Stalin's tyranny still exists today.

But to start the story of the Soviet General Staff we have to go back sixty years to the Russian Imperial General Staff, from which it took its roots. The old Russian Imperial General Staff before the First World War was so closely modelled on the Prussian that it formed almost a replica. Even the teaching of strategy and tactics in the Nikolaevsky War Academy (the Russian Staff College) was based on direct trans-lations from German published works.[2] The General Staff of the new Red Army, called originally the field staff and then the army staff, con-tinued to be strongly influenced by German ideas and organisation. It could hardly have been otherwise, for the first chief of staff, Lebedev, had been a former tsarist general staff officer and a major-general of the Moskovsky Foot Guards; his deputy, Shaposhnikov, had been a former colonel of the general staff; and many of the instructors at the new Red Army schools had been former tsarist military lecturers.[3] In this way many of the old tsarist traditions, and in particular this awe and aping of all things German, continued without a break into the 1920s and 1930s. This expressed itself in a fervid desire for contacts and ex-changes with the German Army, which came to fruition in the Krasin-von Schleicher talks and in Rapallo and the secret agreement whereby the Germans sent industrial and military missions to Russia and had the

65

ten-year use of Soviet schools and training grounds. This exchange had to be paid for by the Germans in ideas and in hard currency.[4]

From 1927 to 1937 the Red Army General Staff formed part of Voroshilov's Commissariat for Military and Naval Affairs, and served as the general staff not only for the Red Army and Air Force, for the Air Force formed part of the Army, but for the Soviet Navy as well. In 1937 the control of the Soviet Navy was removed to a separate Commissariat for the Navy, firstly under Smirnov and then under Kuznetsov, with its own naval operations staff, although this in fact remained subordinate to the general staff in all matters of policy and co-ordination.[5]

During the 1930s the only source of all authority within the Soviet Union was of course Stalin, and Stalin alone directed Soviet home and foreign policy and military affairs. The extent of his power and activities and the closeness of his control were not known either inside or outside the USSR for, unlike Lenin, Stalin was content to rule from the shadows. Stalin was Secretary-General and head of the Communist Party Politburo, but he held no government post. Kalinin was President, Molotov, as Chairman of the Cabinet, was Prime Minister and Voroshilov was Minister for Defence; in reality all of them were Stalin's pliant puppets.[6] The Foreign Ministers, Chicherin and Litvinov, were of no account; they were not even in the Politburo.

The Chief of General Staff's influence with Stalin, if indeed he had any, did not depend on Voroshilov, his nominal superior. For, although Voroshilov wore the uniform of a Marshal of the Soviet Union, he had no claim at all to being a professional soldier, and Stalin had a very low opinion of his military ability; nor is it likely that Voroshilov's views on diplomatic matters would have carried any weight. Stalin worked directly not only with the Chief of General Staff but also with the heads of staff directorates, for Stalin liked to have his information first hand. Stalin's relationship with his senior staff and commanders was personal and close, and he would invite them regularly to supper at his country house, where the military talks would continue far into the night. The dictator was a member of Molotov's Committee on Defence and Voroshilov's Main Military Council of the Red Army; all decisions taken there depended entirely on Stalin.[7]

In tracing the background and the aims of the foreign policy of the Soviet Union, one has no Politburo protocols, no Moscow archives, on which to rest one's case. But one does have the very informative Russian language press and literature as a source, and using this, together with precedent and probability as a yardstick, it is a fairly easy task to unravel the apparent contradictions that confronted and confused Western statesmen in the 1930s. Few, if any, of these statesmen realised that Stalin was the only master, and that Molotov, Litvinov, Voroshilov and the Red Army spokesmen rarely uttered any words other than those put into their mouths by the dictator. That there were many contradictions there can be no doubt. The words used by Soviet spokesmen were often deliberately false, mischievous and provocative, or were kites flown in search of a reaction. And it was Stalin's way to encourage the fiction that he himself was not in complete control, and that there were two or more opposing factions within the Politburo and the government.[8] At the centre of this intricate web of lies and deception was Stalin's hand controlling the many threads; for Stalin was a master not of ideas but of timing and manipulation. What matters most is not what was said but when and why it was said.

During the 1920s and early 1930s the Soviet long-term aim was the re-annexation of territories formerly in the Empire and the claiming of those lands populated by separatist groups of Ukrainians and Belorussians. But the Soviet Union still feared foreign intervention and, because the Red Army was weak, Moscow did not dare to interfere openly with Finland, the Baltic States, Poland or Rumania. In 1927 Stalin was advocating revolution and subversion in the capitalist states, and the Comintern and Soviet embassies sought to exploit any frictions abroad, whether these were international, national, political, ethnic or social. Germany was encouraged to flout the military provisions of Versailles in order that it might come into conflict with France and Britain. On the other hand any hint of a Franco-German *entente,* i.e. Locarno or the entry of Germany into the League of Nations, was regarded in Moscow as a threat against itself; and the Soviet Union became even more uneasy when, in 1933, influential London politicians voiced their support of Hitler as a bulwark against communism, one of them going so far as to encourage German expansion eastwards at the expense of Russia.

Stalin met this situation in his own way, by indiscriminately signing pacts with all and sundry, with the Baltic States, Poland, Germany, France, Czechoslovakia, Turkey, Persia and Afghanistan; 'paper ramparts' one writer called them. It is remarkable that one who would so readily dishonour any agreement should have attached so much importance to these scraps of paper. The rise of Hitler's Germany could have pushed the Soviet Union into the French camp, but it did not. For Stalin not only shared with his own general staff the exaggerated respect for German military efficiency and power, but, as we shall see later, he actually reinforced it in his soldiers' minds. He decided to back both horses and Moscow began to speak with two voices, Molotov and Stalin being among those conciliatory to Hitler's Germany while Litvinov, the Foreign Minister, favoured the French.

Stalin's power and the control of the communist police state were such that, even long before the purges, senior Red Army commanders and staff feared their own shadowing commissars and avoided contact with foreigners.[9] But, on occasions, some did express views to distinguished visitors; a few of these views, perhaps, were genuine opinions, bravely or indiscreetly voiced; but for the most part the generals appear to have acted under instructions, using words that were designed to convey an impression or elicit a response. In 1928, for example, Voroshilov told von Blomberg that the Russo-German collaboration was a policy that *he* had pushed through against some opposition, an obvious hint to the Germans that they should not take too much for granted. Both Voroshilov and Tukhachevsky advocated what they called a Russo-German preventive war against Poland, and in 1930 Uborevich told Heye that the USSR was ready to slaughter the Poles and, together with Germany, partition Poland once more. These Stalin-inspired words were probably crude political feelers.

In 1933 Moscow ordered the closing of the German training establishments in Russia; at the time the German military attaché reported that the action was political and against the inclination of the Red Army General Staff. This was probably true. And when the first French military attaché arrived in Moscow in April it was Stalin himself who arranged the political and military reception in his honour. In May 1934 the Soviet Union signed with France the Pact of Mutual Assistance and a similar pact with Czechoslovakia, this latter being dependent on French assistance to the victim of the attack. The USSR then joined the League of Nations.

About a month later, when the news arrived in Moscow of Hitler's Röhm putsch, Stalin had a meeting in his office attended by Berzin, the head of the intelligence directorate of the General Staff. Afterwards Berzin told his deputy Krivitsky that Stalin had come to the conclusion that Hitler was the real master of Germany and would remain so. From this time onwards, said Krivitsky, Stalin determined to come to terms with Germany.[10] It was shortly after this that the Finnish Ambassador in Moscow gave his opinion that 'Russia would end in half an hour the agreement with France if only Germany would sign a pact'.

The scene was now set for Munich. The first of the Chiefs of Staff, following on Lebedev and Frunze, was undoubtedly the most controversial. Tukhachevsky came from the hereditary nobility, beginning his military service as a second lieutenant in the Semenovsky Foot Guards in late 1913. He was taken prisoner fifteen months later. When he returned to Russia in 1918 he immediately joined the Bolshevik Party.[11] A year later this second lieutenant, virtually without military training or experience, was commanding an army group, a post normally reserved for a field-marshal or a full general, because, and here I quote his commissar Ordzhonikidze, 'he had read Clausewitz'.[12] Tukhachevsky became Chief of General Staff for three years from 1925 and then, in 1931, returned as a deputy to Voroshilov with a special responsibility for armaments. Many Western writers, possibly with little knowledge of the man or his work, have called Tukhachevsky 'brilliant'. A better informed historian noted him as 'the brain behind the modernisation of the Red Army'. I am inclined to qualify even this description since, in my view, it takes insufficient account of Stalin's controlling hand — for better or for worse — over rearmament and the creation of the industrial arms base.

If Tukhachevsky's military experience and ability were of a high order this is not immediately apparent in his writing; and no educated soldier could have been so obsessed with politics as a means of waging war. Although he could, when at his ease, speak fluently and confidently, using the cultured tones and the spontaneous courtesy of the Semenovsky Foot Guards, too often he tried to shine by adopting an aggressive and destructive attitude to the ideas and works of minds more creative than his own, expressing his opinions abrasively and often violently, so incurring the personal dislike of others. He had an agile and lively brain and was considered by some to be an ambitious adventurer.[13]

When in 1936 Tukhachevsky visited Paris, at the French invitation, he appeared quite sure of himself. But he caused the greatest surprise to his listeners when he publicly attacked any attempt to align the Soviet Union with collective security, telling a journalist that the Germans were already invincible. These views were undoubtedly Stalin's although whether the volatile Tukhachevsky had been instructed to give them an airing in this particular fashion is another matter. And he told the Rumanian Minister that henceforth Rumania should look to Germany for rescue — presumably from the Soviet Union.[14] According to *Abwehr* sources Tukhachevsky tried to contact the émigré Russian General Miller. Miller himself was being shadowed by another émigré, the former General Skoblin, subsequently thought to have been in touch with the NKVD or SD, or both.

Shortly afterwards Benes, the President of Czechoslovakia, claimed
to have had knowledge of military intelligence traffic passing between
Berlin and Moscow through the Soviet Embassy in Prague and, believing
the Red Army was in touch with Berlin, he passed this information to
Stalin. It is said that Benes's action was based on Skoblin's reports,
deliberately fed to the Czechs, that Tukhachevsky was in touch with
the German General Staff and was intending a *coup d'état* in Russia.
Some believe that Hitler set Heydrich to work to embellish Skoblin's
information in order to destroy the Soviet High Command; others that
Stalin and the NKVD fed in the information to Paris or Belin in order
to make use of it against Tukhachevsky when the reports went the full
circle and came back to Moscow. It should, however, be remembered
that Tukhachevsky when in Paris had shown a little too much warmth
in his opinions, so that the émigrés and the Germans surmised, not
unnaturally, that Tukhachevsky was a powerful political figure in the
Soviet Union — or shortly aimed to become so. This surmise would
undoubtedly have found its way back to Stalin. In any event the outcome was fatal for Tukhachevsky.

In 1938 Russia was isolated from the rest of Europe: its relations
with Britain and Germany were bad; after Tukhachevsky's visit, the
French might have been excused their doubts regarding Russia's sin-
cerity about collective security and mutual aid. Then came the Munich
crisis. The Red Army did not mobilise and nothing appeared in the
Russian press to warn the Soviet population that war was in any way
imminent. And when Czechoslovakia did mobilise, the mobilisation was
condemned in *Pravda* as a provocation that relieved Russia of any
responsibility to come to the Czechs' aid. And, as Beloff has said, 'Since
the USSR chose appeasement in 1939, would it not have done so in
1938? The question must be asked even if it can receive no conclusive
answer.' 'Fellow travellers who shared the communists' convictions
without, however, holding a party card, sat comfortably in a train
labelled "Collective Security" pulled by a Russian engine with honest
Maxim Litvinov at the controls.' These words are Richard Bennett's,
not mine.

The Chief of General Staff from 1931 to 1937 was Egorov, a former
tsarist lieutenant-colonel of the Bendersky Regiment, a man of no
apparent outstanding ability who seems to have owed his advancement
to his close association with Stalin from 1919 to 1921. This did not
save him, however, at the time of the purges, for he was arrested in
1937 and died four years later, presumably shot. His fault is unknown.
Before becoming a Bolshevik he had been a Left Socialist

Revolutionary; later he was a military attaché in China; both of these were sufficient causes of offence to Stalin.

In March 1939 Lithuania, under pressure from Germany, returned the border strip of Memelland that it had seized in 1923, and in the same month German troops occupied Czechoslovakia. The British and French governments, in an attempt to establish a *ne plus ultra* line as a bar to German aggression, guaranteed the territories of Poland and Rumania. Churchill, convinced that the Soviet Union was a potential ally of reliability that would fight Poland's battles in Eastern Europe, was exhorting the Chamberlain Government that the USSR should be brought into a military alliance with France and Britain and the Baltic States.[15] With this in view, exploratory talks began in Moscow in mid-April between the British Ambassador and Litvinov. Almost immediately afterwards, the Kremlin opened parallel though secret negotiations in Berlin. At the beginning of May Litvinov was dropped as Foreign Minister in favour of Molotov, Stalin's henchman and crony.

Poland and Rumania both refused to have Red Army troops within their frontiers, and the Baltic States rejected any guarantee that included the Soviet Union as a signatory. The Moscow talks with Britain and France made little headway. Then, in late July, Stalin suggested a military convention to discuss joint military plans in case of war against Germany. Why he should have done so is unclear, but it would appear, from the way the military talks were subsequently conducted, that he was intent on seeking information about the military resources of the western allies. The talks were attended by Voroshilov, who merely pressed demands for the entry of the Red Army into Poland and Rumania, and by Shaposhnikov and Loktionov who presented what was said to be the Soviet military picture, together with a proposal to use a graduated scale of percentages of the Soviet armed strength against Germany according to the different political situations that might arise.[16] Wars are not fought in such a fashion. On 17 August Voroshilov told the allied missions that he regarded a European war as a certainty. The British Army representative has said, in retrospect, that 'it seemed to have been merely a question of who – Germany or the western allies – could make the best offer in the shortest time'. In any event the Soviet double game had little to do with the preservation of peace.

On 23 August 1939 came the von Ribbentrop-Molotov pact partitioning Poland (which was to be invaded by both German and Red Army troops) and giving Stalin a curiously undefined freedom to manage the affairs of central and south-east Europe as he thought fit.[17] All shades of world political opinion, from the Communist apologists on the left, to Winston Churchill, the berater of Chamberlain, on the right, have contrived to excuse Stalin by blaming as 'Munich appeasers' the British Conservative Government of the time. There is, on the other hand, a contrary view that regards such an attitude as extraordinarily naive. Commentators who share this contrary view argue that the Soviet Union was motivated by its own interest and its own security, not collective security, and that its peaceful intentions should be judged by its subsequent partition of Poland, its war against Finland and the annexation of the Baltic States, Bessarabia and Bukovina. And of course they have logic on their side.

Even so, Stalin should not be judged too harshly because he was unwilling, as he said himself, 'to pull other people's chestnuts out of the fire'. He acted solely in what he judged to be Russian Communist interests, for the Germans held out the tempting offer of a free hand in eastern Europe in return for the expenditure of a little of Molotov's ink, while the western allies offered a long, dangerous and bloodletting war, without an inch of anybody else's territory in exchange.

But there is another and more sinister aspect to the Soviet manoeu-vrings. On 27 August, before the invasion of Poland, both Voroshilov and the Soviet Ambassador in Warsaw held out a promise of benevolent neutrality and war supplies if Poland should fight, and this at a time when the Soviet decision had already been taken to invade the country.[18] This duplicity was presumably intended to ensure that Poland should not capitulate to Germany as Czechoslovakia had done, and that the Anglo-French should be forced into war with Germany; for we know from Kuznetsov's account that Molotov regarded it in Moscow's interests that Germany should be heavily bogged down in fighting in the west, so leaving the Soviet Union free to pursue what Molotov called its own business in the east.[19] In the event, Stalin was of course shortsighted in placing any trust in the Ribbentrop scrap of paper, but he was not to know that the military might of France would collapse in a matter of weeks. Even as late as March and April 1941 the Soviet Union deliberately attempted to incite both Turkey and Yugo-slavia into war with Germany; the Soviet offer of military assistance to the Yugoslavs was hastily withdrawn when they tried to invoke it. For it is no fallacy that Stalin aimed to prosper from other people's wars.

Shaposhnikov, the Chief of General Staff in 1940, had been ailing and had given way to a younger man, Meretskov, the Director of Training. After a few months Meretskov proved unsatisfactory both to Stalin and to Timoshenko, the new Minister for Defence, and was returned to his previous appointment. Stalin might have chosen one of the directorate heads of the General Staff, Malandin or Vatutin, to be the new Chief of Staff, but instead he accepted Timoshenko's suggestion that Zhukov, a former tsarist cavalry non-commissioned officer, be appointed to the post; Zhukov was not staff trained and had no staff experience, and he, too, was to prove unsatisfactory.

It was during Zhukov's tenure of office from February to July 1941 that Stalin became aware of the German troop concentrations on the frontier. He became irritable, unnerved and frightened. Stalin told Zhukov that if the Germans attacked the Soviet Union, Soviet troops would be unable to stop the break-in, for the *Wehrmacht* had more fighting experience and greater technical ability than the Red Army; and he expressed himself so forcefully that the Soviet generals said afterwards that they 'were absolutely staggered by these words as if they had been sedition'.[20]

As Chiefs of General Staff, Meretskov and Zhukov were of no significance. As soon as the war started Shaposhnikov returned to his old post yet again. Shaposhnikov was undoubtedly the most knowledgeable and probably the most influential of all the Chiefs of General Staff. The son of a minor civil servant, commissioned into the Turkestan Rifles — a non-Russian regiment — in 1903, he was taken only four years later into the General Staff Academy at St Petersburg where he graduated in 1910, having become a staunch advocate of the German command and staff system. During the First World War he was successively chief intelligence officer of an army and a front, chief of staff to a corps and then commander of a Caucasian grenadier division. He voluntarily joined the Red Army as chief of intelligence and then deputy chief of staff.

General Knox, the head of the British Military Mission in Russia from 1914 to 1917, knew Shaposhnikov well and considered him an outstandingly able officer. Von Blomberg, who met Shaposhnikov in 1928, described him as 'well groomed . . . the English officer type . . . reserved, logical and systematic with a strong grip on direction and management'. Vasilevsky, Golikov and Shtemenko, who worked under Shaposhnikov for a number of years, including the first two years of the Second World War, said of him that he excelled in the operational and strategic sphere and was an absolute master of warfare at the highest level. He had an enormous fund of military knowledge, a lucid brain and excellent memory and spoke with great assurance. He was always correct and polite to all, yet he was very exacting in spite of his old-fashioned and courteous way of speaking. He was, said Golikov, a great man, liked and respected by all, remarkable for his discipline, integrity, modesty, benevolence, humanity, his sensitive nature and decency. Apparently he was also liked by Stalin. But although Shaposhnikov lived on close terms with the dictator, Shaposhnikov himself was, as Hilger noted, extremely wary in Stalin's presence, and, like everyone in the dictator's circle, he was often the butt of his anger. Unlike Tukhachevsky, Shaposhnikov avoided contact with foreigners; he was conservative and made no claims to have discovered a new revolutionary method of waging war; he was politically neutral and he maintained the military point of view to the exclusion of the political factor. During the 1930s and early 1940s he reconstructed the General Staff, reintroducing many of the better features of the old Russian Imperial General Staff.

Shaposhnikov had written a three-volume work which appeared in 1927, a work probably written before Stalin emerged as the sole dictator, called 'The Brain of the Army', describing future war and the place of the General Staff; in this work he improved on the earlier German and French conceptions of total war. He wrote:

> Future wars will be on a vast scale involving the struggle of whole peoples in arms. It is essential that political, economic and military planning should be included under the whole war effort. Since war is a continuation of policy by other means, then the General Staff, the Foreign Office and diplomats, and the chiefs of the machinery of state only defeat their common purpose if each pursues a separate political aim. Diplomacy does not abandon its role because war has begun. The state in all its totality makes war, and collective and unified action is essential. The military directives issued to the General Staff should be an expression of the collective will and the common purpose of the government in pursuit of its political objectives. The General Staff would not therefore be at the mercy of a conflict of aims and competing groups, but would carry out its basic function of preparing for a war that it would direct militarily, and it would remain linked to the policy-making centres of government without degenerating into a restricted and isolated military organ.

The soldier Shaposhnikov desired from his government unified and coordinated direction, and he certainly got it from Stalin, for by July 1941 Stalin, in additon to this many other posts, was head of the Politburo, the Cabinet, the State Defence Committee and the War Council of the High Command, as well as being Defence Minister, Commander-in-Chief of the Armed Forces and Commander-in-Chief of the Red Army. And he kept these many appointments all through the war.

In some respects Stalin and Shaposhnikov were made for each other — a complementary pair. Many of Shaposhnikov's views undoubtedly rubbed off on the dictator. Yet it should not, of course, be supposed that Stalin was necessarily guided or influenced by the General Staff, even on military matters, for he regarded the General Staff merely as his executive. Its advice might or might not be asked for. As soon as Stalin had made up his mind, that was an end to all discussion, for everyone lived in mortal dread of him. The purges of the 1930s that had decimated not only the Soviet High Command but the population of the USSR in every walk of life had left more than an indelible impression, and the arrests and shootings continued, although on a reduced scale, throughout the remainder of the dictator's life. When Shaposhnikov handed over his office in the middle of the Second World War, it was to Vasilevsky, a former tsarist officer trained and moulded in the Shaposhnikov school.

Finally, there can be no doubt that Communism under Lenin and Stalin, particularly under Stalin, arrived at a clear understanding of the place of diplomacy and war in the furtherance of its aims. The subject of this chapter, that international order is firmly established in peace and breaks down in time of war, or that the waging of war displaces diplomacy, is a western conception entirely foreign to Communist thought. For the Soviet aim was to cause the collapse of both national and international order in times of peace. Nor did Moscow believe that war causes any break in diplomacy or that there was any clear delineation between diplomacy and armed conflict, for the long-term objectives remained the same in peace and war.

Notes

1. The KGB, originally the GPU and OGPU, was reconstituted as the GUGB in 1934 and subordinate to the NKVD. It was redesignated as the NKGB in 1941.
2. Shaposhnikov, *Akademiia General 'nogo Shtaba*, from Voenno-*Istoricheskii Zhurnal*, 9/66, pp. 73 et seq.
3. Budenny, *Proidennyi Put'*, Vol. 2, pp. 14, 19 et seq; Meretskov, *Na Sluzhbe Narodu*, p. 167.
4. Cf. Muller-Hillebrand, *Das Heer 1933-45*, Vol. 1, p. 17 and n.
5. *Armiia Sovetskaia*, p. 116; *50 Let Vooryzhennykh Sil*, pp. 198-9.
6. Cf. Bazhanov, *Stalin – Der Rote Diktator*, pp. 17-25, 29-34, 94-5; also *Pobeg iz Nochi*, Kontinent No. 8, 1976.

7. Meretskov, *Na Sluzhbe Narodu,* pp. 168-9.
8. A belief apparently shared by Churchill, even as late as 1944. See Churchill, *Triumph and Tragedy,* Vol. 6, pp. 207-8.
9. Cf. von Manstein, *Aus einem Soldatenleben,* pp. 140-3.
10. Krivitsky, *I was Stalin's Agent,* p. 114.
11. Todorsky, *Marshal Tukhachevsky,* pp. 12-24.
12. Budenny, *Proidennyi Put',* Vol. 1, pp. 434-6.
13. Barmine, *Memoirs of a Soviet Diplomat,* pp. 302-4.
14. Cf. Erickson, *The Soviet High Command,* p. 388 et seq.
15. Churchill, *The Gathering Storm,* Vol. 1, p. 242
16. Bezymensky, *Sonderakte Barbarossa,* pp. 47-127.
17. *Nazi-Soviet Relations 1939-41,* pp. 78 and 157; Beloff, *The Foreign Policy of Soviet Russia,* Vol. 2, p. 278, n.2.
18. *Polish-German and Polish-Soviet Relations, 1933-39,* No. 163, p. 183.
19. As reported by Zhdanov-Kuznetsov, *Voenno-Istoricheskii Zhurnal,* 9/65, pp. 73 et seq.
20. Bagramian, *Voenno-Istoricheskii Zhurnal,* 1/67, p. 56.

5 THE ITALIAN GENERAL STAFF AND THE COMING OF THE SECOND WORLD WAR

John Whittam

On 23 November 1940 von Rintelen, German military attaché in Rome, sent a gloomy appraisal of the Mediterranean situation to his superiors in Berlin. Italy's attack on Greece, which the Führer himself described as *'entsetzlich und dumm'*, had led to humiliating retreats after only a month's fighting. In North Africa, Graziani was sitting outside Sidi Barrani allowing the British time to organise a counter-offensive, while throughout the Mediterranean the Royal Navy and the RAF dominated the sea and the sky from their bases in Alexandria, Malta and Gibraltar. His conclusion was that Germany would have to intervene to prevent her axis partner from complete disaster.[1] He was reproved by von Brauchitsch, the Chief of Army Command, for being unduly pessimistic and failing to provide 'moral support for the Italian military authorities', but within a few weeks the Luftwaffe was operating from bases in Sicily and Rintelen's suggestion had been incorporated into Hitler's War Directive No. 22 of 11 January 1941.[2] This marked an important turning point in the war, and but for the previous directive of 18 December, Operation Barbarossa, could have been decisive.

Also on 23 November and not unconnected with Rintelen's report — Roberto Farinacci, the influential ex-secretary of the fascist party, launched an attack on the Italian general staff in his newspaper *Il Regime Fascista.*[3] Never an admirer of Marshal Pietro Badoglio, who had been chief of the general staff since 1925, Farinacci welcomed this opportunity to contribute to the disgrace of a man he despised for being a Piedmontese conservative, a traditionalist officer, a mason, a francophile and an ambitious careerist who received honours and rewards from a regime he had never wholeheartedly supported. Badoglio had somehow survived Mussolini's frequent 'changing of the guard', had won glory in Libya and Abyssinia, and had established himself in a seemingly impregnable position as the most prestigious military figure in Italy. The Greek fiasco, following the invasion of 28 October 1940, gave Farinacci and all Badoglio's enemies the opportunity they had been waiting for.

The disasters in Albania prompted Mussolini to cast about for a scapegoat. Visconti Prasca, the general commanding the troops, and

Jacomoni, the Governor of Albania, were too close to Ciano and too
obscure to be suitable candidates for this role. The chief of the general
staff seemed the obvious choice, particularly as the Germans had been
pressing for his removal since the Innsbrück meeting with Keitel on 15
November.[4] The relationship between the king and Badoglio was
extremely cool and in any case Victor Emmanuel III had never inter-
vened vigorously on behalf of anyone or anything for the past forty
years. So Farinacci was unloosed.

Badoglio fought back, threatening to resign if Farinacci refused to
withdraw his remarks. No public apology appeared and Badoglio
handed the Duce his letter of resignation on 26 November. According
to Ciano it was at this meeting that Mussolini confronted Badoglio with
a written statement from Alessandro Pavolini, the minister for popular
culture, recounting a conversation held a few days earlier. Badoglio was
supposed to have said:

> There is no doubt that Jacomoni and Visconti Prasca have a large
> share of the responsibility in the Albanian affair, but the real blame
> must be sought elsewhere. It lies entirely with the Duce's command.
> This is a command which he, the Duce, cannot hold. Let him leave
> everything to us, and when things go wrong let him punish those
> responsible.[5]

Mussolini hesitated before finally accepting the resignation, and
Badoglio went to the king on 3 December offering to withdraw it, but
it was too late. The following day the Duce made it clear that the
marshal's services were no longer required, and on 6 December Ugo
Cavallero was appointed in his place.[6] Badoglio retired, perhaps already
seeing himself as an Italian Pétain keeping himself in reserve for some
future national catastrophe.[7] The campaign of vilification which had
developed in fascist circles was called off by Mussolini before it became
too destructive and accusations of treachery against Badoglio were
quietly dropped.

During November and December 1940 most of the questions discussed in this paper were raised and hotly debated. That many of them
are still controversial is evident from a study of the now extensive literature on the subject of Italy and her involvement in the Second World
War. Even if the military archives were made accessible, it is doubtful
whether they would provide either easy answers or different answers to
the basic problems concerning responsibility for policies and their
implementation. That Italy was unprepared for war in 1939-40 seems

incontrovertible but perhaps requires a brief analysis. Historians also seem agreed that there was a growing gap between ends and means in the 1930s, the pursuit of a grandiose foreign policy without the necessary military or industrial resources to back it up.

Involved with this issue is the fascinating topic of Mussolini's systematic use or misuse of bluff, *'una politica bluffistica e grottesca'* in the words of Giorgio Rochat.[8] In this realm of rhetoric and deception, which has recently been so devastatingly exposed by Denis Mack Smith,[9] it is sometimes apparent that a surer guide than Clausewitz — with his famous dictum — would be Lewis Carroll. The editor of *Il Populo D'Italia* was so convinced by the power of words that he came to believe that even foreign policy and military objectives were attainable by the skilful deployment of an army of journalists rather than by the more orthodox formations.

But the armed forces still had a crucial role to play in lending credibility to the Duce's propaganda. Once this central proposition is grasped even the most unbelievable events begin to have a certain inner logic of their own. It is within this bizarre framework that the question of the responsibility of Mussolini, of Badoglio and the general staff, of the chiefs of staff and under-secretaries, of the three armed services, and of the fascist regime itself, must all be assessed. Two final problems which were prominent in the acrimonious exchanges of November-December 1940 concern the strategy to be adopted by Italy in view of her geographical position and her domestic and diplomatic requirements, and the nature and purpose of her commitment to Nazi Germany.

Whatever eventual conclusions can be drawn, Mussolini was filled with gloom after the polemical exchanges with Badoglio and temporarily felt that his grand design had failed. As news of reverses on all fronts flowed in, he admitted: 'I must nevertheless recognise that the Italians of 1914 were better than these. It is not flattering for the regime, but that's how it is.' He began to develop this theme on the following day, Christmas Eve 1940. In the words of Ciano's diary:

> It is snowing. The Duce looks out of the window and is glad that it is snowing. 'This snow and cold are very good,' he says. 'In this way our good-for-nothing Italians, this mediocre race, will be improved. One of the principal reasons I have desired the reafforestation of the Apennines has been to make Italy colder and snowier.'[10]

There was nothing wrong with the grand design, it was just that the

Italians were unworthy of it. Ciano, who followed his father-in-law's thought patterns more closely than he dared to admit, wrote a few weeks later about the rout in Albania:

> Greece was a political masterpiece; we succeeded in isolating that country so that it had to fight against us all alone. Only the Italian army failed us completely.[11]

Not for the first time, the foreign minister had not only missed the point but got his facts wrong as well.

The issues and problems outlined above are so interconnected that it is difficult to isolate them and deal systematically with each one. Italian preparedness for war, for instance, is intimately linked to the question of Mussolini's responsibility for the disasters of 1940-3. In turn, this cannot be evaluated without reference to the role of military advisers, the type of war being envisaged or the strategy to be pursued. However, as Mussolini said in early 1940 when informed that the army would not be ready for years, 'faremo quello che potremo', we must do what we can.[12] After he had been removed from power in July 1943 and re-established by the Nazis in the puppet republic of Salo, Mussolin wrote a book in which he claimed, amongst other things, that he had been misled by the military, that the inefficiency of the armed forces was a complete revelation to him and that he had been most reluctant to assume supreme command in 1940.[13] In his stimulating book, *Too Serious a Business* (London and Berkeley, California, 1975), Professor D.C. Watt comes very close on three occasions to accepting, at least in part, Mussolini's apologia. After explaining that the Duce failed to give any long-term directives to the chiefs of staff, and that they in turn never demanded them, he writes:

> This continued right up until the Italian entry into the war. And deprived of strategic directives the generals could only express their anxieties in the void, or to their would-be allies. The German audience for Marshal Pariani during his visit to the country in the summer of 1938, the German military attaché in Rome, the German participants in the staff talks of April and June 1939 heard far more of these anxieties than Mussolini did.

This could give the wrong impression. General Pariani was chief of army staff and under-secretary at the war ministry between October 1936 and October 1939 and throughout this period — indeed since 1933 —

Mussolini himself was the war minister. It is true that Pariani's philosophical theories of war, including his *'tattica dell'acqua'* and his Bergsonian belief in 'spirit' and 'faith' (*'e quando c'e la fede, c'e la forza animatrice per qualsiasi impresa'*) earned him so much ridicule that Federzoni described him as a man 'who had lost all sense of reality', but it would be unfair and incorrect to argue that he complained to the Germans far more regularly than to Mussolini.[14] Indeed, in the staff talks in April 1939 mentioned in the quotation, Pariani left Keitel with the impression that Italy was planning a localised war with France in the immediate future.[15] It was Keitel who drew his own conclusions about the efficiency of the Italian armed forces.

That Mussolini was kept informed by his under-secretaries is well documented. After the signing of the Pact of Steel, it was Mussolini who drew up the famous Cavallero Memorandum explaining to Hitler why he was unprepared for war prior to 1942. One of Professor Watt's sources (and one used for this paper) is Carlo de Biase, who dislikes general staffs and particularly the Italian general staff. He prefaces the part of his book dealing with the interwar period with a quotation from Carlo Silvestri: 'The only military operation serious planned by the general staff during the war has been the arrest of Mussolini.'[16] At the risk of a dreadful pun it must be admitted that Biase is biased. In another passage, Professor Watt rightly points to the rigid separation of the three armed services in Italy and to the absence of any machinery resembling a combined chiefs of staffs committee. He continues:

> Mussolini's own complete lack of either staff or expertise meant that the approach of war in Europe found the Italian armed forces militarily unprepared, without any plans save theoretical staff exercises prepared by the staffs of the three services virtually in a vacuum. Since there were no war plans, there were no plans for industry. Mussolini himself seems to have remained in the profoundest ignorance of all this, convinced by his own rhetoric that all was well with the forces of the inheritor of the mantle of Pompey and Caesar. This alone can explain the extraordinary ignorance he was to display in the summer of 1939, having signed the Pact of Steel . . . In 1939, according to the diaries of Count Ciano, his son-in-law, he had been reduced to instructing the Fascist prefects of each region to make a visual count of the aircraft on the military airfields in their regions as the only way of learning the real strength of the Italian Air Force.[17]

It will be shown later that the Duce was not in the profoundest ignorance. That he failed to act on the information received is another question. As for the reference to Ciano, it was the foreign minister who put forward this suggestion for checking the figures presented by Valle, the under-secretary for air (Mussolini was, of course, the air minister). 'I advised him', wrote Ciano, 'to start an investigation through the prefects: count the planes in the hangars and then add them up. This should not be an impossible undertaking.'[18] Whether Mussolini took this advice or not is unknown. The likelihood is that he was unconcerned about the exact figure provided the world continued to believe that his aircraft could 'blot out the sun'.

There was a similar episode back in 1933. On 5 November 1933 Mussolini decided to remove Italo Balbo from the air ministry where he had been in control since 1926, first as under-secretary then as minister. Balbo had raised the prestige of the Italian air force by encouraging it to participate in various air races, including formation flights across the Atlantic, and by doing his best to ensure that its aircraft won. As Balbo's popularity grew so did Mussolini's suspicion, but in any case he had decided to take over the three ministries himself, thus reverting to the situation of 1925-9. To prevent Balbo from organising some sort of protest, the Duce wrote him a second letter on 12 November. In it he reminded Balbo that he had declared that the air force possessed a total of 3,125 aircraft whereas in fact there were only 911 *dal punto di vista bellico*. However he concluded, 'I hasten to add that I consider this situation to be satisfactory.'[19]

This short letter reveals three things. Mussolini, even in the period 1929-33 when he had temporarily relinquished control over the three service ministries, was quite capable of finding out exactly what was going on. Secondly, he was unmoved by the discrepancy he had discovered, did nothing to improve the situation, and was probably only concerned lest the information leaked out. Finally, he was prepared to use this whole episode to blackmail Balbo into silence. The success of the Duce's impressive use of bluff depended on the complicity, willing or otherwise, of the entire military hierarchy. In private, they could, and often did, express their fears and hesitations, but any public dispute was absolutely forbidden.

One final passage from Professor Watt's book perhaps requires comment. After admitting that the army chiefs 'had done their level best in the spring of 1940 to warn Mussolini of the deplorable state of Italy's army', he proceeds to condemn the general staff for the failure of the Greek war.

But the illusion that Italy could stage a war limited to eleven divisions, of which only seven could actually take part in the operations against a Greek enemy whose full armed forces amounted to three times that figure, and whose divisions were one third as strong again as their own, was the contribution of the Italian General Staff alone.[20]

Unless General Soddu can be said to represent the entire general staff, this is far too sweeping a condemnation. Apart from Soddu, under-secretary for war and deputy chief of the general staff, the staff officers were deliberately kept on the sidelines and only called in to sanction decisions which had already been agreed upon and accepted by Mussolini. The men who made the decisions were Ciano, who always regarded Albania as a kind of private fief, Jacomoni, General Visconti Prasca, and Mussolini himself. On 12 October 1940 Mussolini expressed his irritation at Hitler's occupation of Rumania and swore to pay him back in his own coin. 'He will find out from the papers that I have occupied Greece.' Ciano then asked him if he had reached an agreement with Badoglio.

'Not yet,' he answers, 'but I shall send in my resignation as an Italian if anyone objects to our fighting the Greeks.' The Duce seems determined to act now. In fact, I believe that the military operation will be useful and easy.[21]

On 14 October, the deputy army chief of staff General Roatta was under the impression that the Greek war had been called off and notified Visconti Prasca accordingly.[22] The following day, however, Mussolini summoned Badoglio, Roatta, Soddu, Visconti Prasca, Jacomoni and Ciano, and ordered them to launch the war on 26 October. Apparently Badoglio did not speak up at this meeting, but two days later he informed Ciano that he and the chiefs of staff were unanimously opposed to such precipitate action.[23] The air and naval chiefs of staff, Pricolo and Cavagnari, must have been particularly perturbed as they had not even been invited to the meeting of 15 October. Badoglio told Soddu that he intended to resign if the Greek invasion went ahead.[24] When he met the Duce, Badoglio failed to carry out his threat and his only achievement was to secure a two-day postponement of the war. On 10 November at a meeting of the chiefs of staff, Badoglio bitterly criticised Mussolini for not involving them properly in the preparations for the Greek war.[25] Without in any way absolving

Badoglio for his rather supine behaviour, this view does seem to be generally accepted. (The various war plans which the staff were asked to devise, dating back to 16 August 1939, will be briefly discussed when Italy's strategic alternatives are examined.)

Two final points concerning responsibility for the Greek war are perhaps worth mentioning. In September 1940, without consulting Badoglio, Mussolini began the demobilisation of 600,000 men.[26] Secondly, at the meeting on 15 October, although the chief of the general staff appears to have given qualified support for the attack on Greece, he did argue in favour of a delay of at least three months, and if more than a limited campaign were contemplated he asked for the deployment of twenty divisions, eleven more than those actually based in Albania at that time.[27]

However unprepared Italy was for a long war — and the Cavallero Memorandum and the gigantic shopping list which Mussolini sent to Hitler on 26 August 1939 provide eloquent proof of this — she should have been capable of waging the 'hundred hours war' against France in June 1940 much more effectively; she should have been able to launch a successful assault against a virtually unprotected Malta, or make a more impressive thrust into Egypt or defeat one of her Balkan neighbours, Yugoslavia or Greece. That she failed to do any of these things is not so much the result of insufficient or defective equipment but rather the legacy of nearly twenty years of fascist rule. Propaganda replaced realistic planning, bombastic speeches and slogans the careful evaluation of strategies. Bluff and the appearance of power became more important than keeping abreast of the latest military developments or expanding the armaments industry. All the belligerents in the Second World War were, in one way or another, unprepared for the type of war they had to fight, all of them at times indulged in bluff, and most of them tried to pursue policies which were over-ambitious in relation to their military resources.

But perhaps Mussolini was the only national leader who seriously expected to achieve his objectives without having to wage war seriously. The succession of defeats between 1940 and 1943 revealed that he had gambled and lost, the stakes being nothing less than his own prestige and the existence of the regime itself. In retrospect, what Rochat has called 'the growing gap year after year between a policy of grandeur and a totally inadequate military preparation' is so grotesque that it is this that makes the Italian example unique.[28] The roots of this policy and the disasters of 1940 lie in the period 1922-5 when fascism was consolidating its hold, with the active assistance of the army leadership.

In the months following Caporetto an *'ideologia del combattentismo'* began to take shape.[29] Serving soldiers and veterans, with a certain amount of government support and civilian approval, began to form associations to safeguard their own interests and to press for the implementation of the lavish promises being showered upon them by politicians eager for them to win the war. *'Terra ai contadini'* was a particularly attractive slogan for an army comprised mainly of peasants from central and southern Italy.[30] There were also offers of pensions, full employment and a home fit for heroes. Indeed, after the war there was to be a new army and a new society. Many officers remained dubious about the implications of all this but saw advantages in being able to control their men in peacetime as in war. The shrewder politicians also saw that the combatants and ex-combatants could, if properly organised, become a decisive political factor in postwar Italy. On 9 February 1919 Mussolini's paper *Il Popolo d'Italia,* which had often criticised the 'garrison spirit' of the Italian army, declared that 'the defeat of Caporetto has also been the defeat of the old militarism. At Vittorio Veneto *la nazione armata* triumphed'. After 1922 this assertion was to be endlessly reiterated by the Duce. As Italy's government struggled with postwar problems between 1918 and 1922, the euphoria rapidly evaporated. Many ex-combatants joined various fasci or the ANC (Associazione Nazionale Combattenti) or became legionaries who followed D'Annunzio to Fiume where they were joined by elements from the regular army — the first serious mutiny in its history and a startling indication of the degree of politicisation which had taken place since 1918.

While all this frenetic activity was taking place, the military leaders grouped around Diaz, who had been commander-in-chief for the final year of the war, and Badoglio, who had successfully escaped the consequences of his deplorable conduct at Caporetto, pursued a policy of masterly inactivity. They were hostile to all those who wished to democratise the army and society. Their basic aim was to restore the old pre-war garrison army and resume their role as guardians of the old social order. For this reason, they were also hostile towards those colleagues who advocated sweeping reforms of the military establishment or even technical innovations. They also prevented the officer corps from following the possibly putschist line adopted by Giardino, Aosta and Pecori Giraldi. They ridiculed new theories of warfare like that being put forward by Douhet, and any schemes involving radical reorganisation of the armed forces. The ephemeral nature of postwar ministries meant that war ministers had insufficient time to promote policies. This

lack of continuity enabled the conservative 'victorious generals' to
block all attempts at reform, although in public they announced their
willingness to collaborate in the creation of a genuine *nazione armata*
provided the officer corps did not suffer.

In the course of 1920 and 1921, the arditi organisation, the futurists
under Marinetti, the ANC, and D'Annunzio's legionaries all grew
weaker and increasingly divided. Many of their members joined
Mussolini's increasingly dynamic and successful fascist movement,
which had gradually shed much of its earlier radicalism and had begun
to act as the praetorian guard of the capitalists and landowners. Ultra-
nationalistic Mussolini and his followers had, from the beginning,
declared their solidarity with the army. The squadristi, the armed
fascists who established a reign of terror in so many parts of Italy,
crushing their socialist and catholic rivals, had gradually won the
support of the army and the state authorities. Financed by capitalists
and landowners (who feared a repeat performance of the events of
1919-20 when workers had occupied factories and peasants had
occupied land while the government merely looked on powerless) and
equipped by the army with firearms and lorries, the fascists proved
irresistible. Town after town fell before them, culminating in the
threatened March on Rome which led the King to offer the premiership
to Mussolini. When Victor Emmanuel had sought the advice of Diaz,
Badoglio and Pecori Giraldi they had affirmed their loyalty and their
willingness to crush the squadristi if so ordered, but they had also
reputedly said: 'The army would do its duty but it would be best not to
put it to the test.'[31]

When, on 17 November 1922, Mussolini sat down on his ministerial
bench flanked by his new ministers of war and of the navy, Diaz and
Thaon di Revel, there was wild applause in the chamber. The whole
theatrical scene is reminiscent of Hitler's Potsdam ceremony over a
decade later. When Diaz left office in April 1924, he proudly announced
that the army had successfully surmounted the crisis which had confronted it in 1922.[32] Diaz was happy to confirm Mussolini's extravagant pronouncements which claimed that the new regime had, since
1922, united army and society and established the *nazione armata,* a
warrior nation in arms. What had actually happened was that Mussolini
had given 'the victorious generals' (those who had successfully claimed
to have contributed to the victory of Vittorio Veneto without being
implicated in the defeat of Caporetto) a free hand in purely military
affairs, and had guaranteed them an honoured and privileged place in
society. In return, they were expected to raise no serious objections to

cuts in the military budget and to pledge their support to the regime, a
support which would lend credibility even to the most outrageous
militaristic posturing on the part of the Duce.

Di Giorgio, succeeding Diaz as war minister at the end of April 1924,
was not prepared to play this passive role. This tempestuous Sicilian
general, who had a most impressive war record, was determined to introduce a reform project even if he had the whole of the army council
against him. In view of the financial stringency, he planned to call up
the annual quota of around 225,000 conscripts but to release most of
them after a basic training period of only four months, the money
saved to be used for the re-equipment and rationalisation of the army.[33]
Predictably this produced a storm of protest and, lacking finesse, Di
Giorgio succeeded in alienating nearly everyone. For the first time since
1918-19 and for the last time during the fascist *ventennio,* the army
was publicly debated in the press and parliament. General Bencivenga, a
persistent advocate of the formation of a small but well equipped and
highly trained 'ever-ready' force of 150,000 men, pressed for the acceptance of his *lancia e scudo* project.[34] General Gandolfo put forward a
similar plan for an elite force of twenty divisions which would be
backed by the Militia which he himself then commanded.[35] The
theories of Douhet and Gatti were also publicised and discussed in
these months before the strict censorship of 1925 ended all such
debates for the next fifteen years.

Although alarmed by the increasing opposition to Di Giorgio's
schemes, Mussolini continued to support him until the spring of 1925.
He was grateful for Di Giorgio's unwavering support during the height
of the Matteotti crisis when the war minister had released 100,000
rifles to the Militia and reaffirmed the army's loyalty to the regime. But
Mussolini's famous speech of 3 January 1925, when he accepted full
responsibility for everything done in the name of fascism and
announced the assumption of dictatorial powers, was followed by a
speech to the senate on 2 April 1925 which was equally significant. By
that date, the hostility of Aosta, Giardino, Caviglia and other generals
towards Di Giorgio, together with the unequivocal opposition of
Farinacci and the fascist hierarchy, had convinced Mussolini that Di
Giorgio and his reform project must be sacrificed. In a bombastic
speech, full of sound and fury but signifying very little, the Duce elec-
trified his audience and at the same time withdrew the controversial
project. Two days later Mussolini himself took over the war ministry
and, in the following weeks, the other two service ministries. The
defeats and humiliations of 1940-3 have their origin in these events.

Because Mussolini was not only the Duce of fascism and prime minister but was also foreign minister and, from November 1926, minister of the interior, he was unable to concentrate on running the service ministries, or indeed to play an active role as supreme co-ordinator. He therefore appointed under-secretaries to act for him, Cavallero for the army, Sirianni for the navy and Bonzani for the air force. While they ran the ministries, chiefs of staff supervised the three services. But to act as his principal military adviser and co-ordinator of the armed forces, Mussolini decided to appoint a general who was nationally well known and respected. His choice fell upon Badoglio, who had been chief of staff between November 1919 and February 1921.

Just before the March on Rome Badoglio had been attacked by the fascist leaders but as early as 4 November 1922 he and Mussolini were publicly reconciled. It seems doubtful to argue, therefore, that Badoglio, who for once had backed the wrong side, 'sought refuge for a time as ambassador in Brazil'.[36] Why he accepted the post still remains a mystery, but it certainly proved to be a fortunate move. By going to Brazil in 1923 Badoglio avoided being implicated in the heated arguments which took place during the Matteotti crisis and the preparation of Di Giorgio's reform project. This was certainly one reason why Mussolini chose him in April 1925. Another, less flattering reason may well have been Mussolini's conviction that he would be more malleable than generals like Giardino or Caviglia. He was also believed to be hostile to any far-reaching military reforms and, in addition, he had a guilty secret which could always be used against him — his implication in the defeat of Caporetto. On 4 May 1925 Badoglio became chief of army staff but he was also appointed to an entirely new post, that of chief of the general staff with vague powers of supervision over the other two services. These two posts, however, were separated in February 1927 when Ferrari was appointed chief of army staff. Badoglio perhaps lost this post as a result of over-reacting to a supposed fascist plot against the king in 1926,[37] but he successfully retained his other post until his dismissal in December 1940.

If his main ambition was to restore the old pre-war garrison army, Badoglio was eminently successful. The so-called 'Mussolini reorganisation' of the army in March 1926 established an army of thirty divisions, each of three regiments. The term of service for conscripts was eighteen months. Badoglio showed little interest in mechanisation and from June 1925 established an effective military censorship which prohibited polemical writing even on technical subjects.[38] That he failed to establish an effective conventional army seems borne out by chief of army staff Ferrari's complaint in January 1928 that he had inherited a force of only twenty-one divisions, all poorly equipped.[39]

On taking over his post as chief of the general staff he made it clear in an interview with the newspaper *Epoca* that he did not intend to enforce any co-ordination of the three services.[40] That he might fail to break down the jealously defended autonomy of the three services is readily understandable, but that he failed even to try is surely reprehensible. Perhaps his passivity can be explained by the knowledge that Mussolini would object to any vigorous reorganisation which might have deprived the Duce of his role as mediator of the three armed services and as the only real intermediary between the army and society. Badoglio's enemies explained his conduct by emphasising his love for the trappings of power and his avarice.

In the late 1920s, when there was no serious threat to the stability of Europe, his *immobilismo* and readiness to accept Mussolini's slogans as substitutes for military preparedness may have been unheroic but it was not disastrous for Italy; but when he continued to pursue this policy in the dangerous 1930s, it was. If he failed to see the threats to Italian security in this period of increasing tension, he was blindly incompetent and unfit to hold high office. If he was aware of the threats — and this seems undeniable — and failed to make any strong protests or resign, then he was clearly Mussolini's accomplice, and must share in the responsibility for the disasters of 1940.

It was amazing that he made no protest when the law of 6 February 1927 setting out his powers as chief of the general staff allocated him only six staff officers.[41] Equally staggering was his acceptance of the office of governor of Libya between 1929 and 1933 while still retaining his post as chief of the general staff. In 1934-5 he was largely ignored by Mussolini and De Bono as they prepared for the Ethiopian war and it was to be a similar story in 1938-40. And this was the man who told the Duce on 3 May 1940 that he would resign if there was any attempt to establish a relationship based on that of Hitler and Keitel![42]

This command structure of 1925 was temporarily modified between 1929 and 1933 when Mussolini divested himself of the service ministries. Even in this brief period the illusion of a mighty concentration of power, military and civilian, was preserved. In an article in 1930 Aldo Valori wrote that Mussolini 'through the chief of general staff, was the supreme moderator and organiser of all the armed forces'. As an ex-combatant and a political leader, the Duce could use his invaluable insight to co-ordinate the energies of the nation and direct her foreign policy.[43] Fascist leaders and military chiefs constantly praised his genius and remarked on the perfect fusion between the military and civilian spheres which had been achieved under fascism. Earlier suggestions for a ministry of defence were now deemed unnecessary and equally superfluous was the creation of a chiefs of staff committee. But when the Duce again resumed control of the service ministries in 1933 he did make one change. His under-secretaries also became chiefs of staff. At least on paper, his control over the armed forces was absolute. As he explained on 29 May 1940, just before the declaration of war, 'My chief of the general staff is Marshal Badoglio. I give him the directives which will be implemented by the three chiefs of staff of the army, navy, and air force.'[44] One fundamental defect of this command system, in peacetime and in war, was Mussolini's inability or unwillingness to issue clear directives based on a realistic appraisal of the military and diplomatic factors involved.

Career diplomats like Baron Guariglia, Salvatore Contarini, Augusto Rosso and Bernardo Attolico advocated a sober realism in the conduct of foreign policy which Mussolini found uncongenial. Italy, wrote Guariglia to Dino Grandi, foreign minister from 1929 to 1932, was

> historically constrained, for intrinsic and obvious reasons, to take its stand first on one side and then on another; to pursue the execution of its aims by cutting from the garment of its different adversaries the material necessary for its own cloak; and to take refuge on rainy days (so long as this cloak was not ready) under the ample and capacious mantle of England.[45]

Apart from the Corfu incident, Mussolini's conduct of foreign policy was relatively restrained even if his pronouncements were not, at least during the first ten years of the regime. The foreign office officials of the Palazzo Chigi succeeded in 'capturing' the fascist quadrumvir Grandi, and later on perhaps half-captured Mussolini's son-in-law Ciano. The Badoglio-Mussolini reorganisation of the army in March 1926, with all its deficiencies, was adequate for an Italy intent upon maintaining a low profile and a defensive posture. But Mussolini increasingly resented a policy of cautious statesmanship with its Locarno pacts, discussions at Geneva and disarmament conferences. Between 1932, when Grandi was dismissed and sent to London, and 1934, the Duce's restlessness began to be translated into action. Roland Sarti has suggested that 'the aggressive foreign policy of fascism after 1934 was perhaps an attempt to prolong the revolutionary image of fascism by military means'.[46]

The dynamism of the new Third Reich was also a major stimulant. The decision to attack Ethiopia, which the career diplomats hoped to present as a localised and limited colonial war, produced its own momentum. The prestige of the regime and Mussolini's position in it became dependent on a triumphant outcome. In the process, Italy alienated Britain and France and came into conflict with the League. Italo-German relations, which had been extremely cool between the abortive coup in Vienna and the formation of the Stresa front, began to improve. Instead of adopting a strong line against Anschluss or German rearmament, Mussolini found himself with little alternative other than rapprochement with Hitler. Because of economic sanctions in 1935, Britain virtually ceased to supply Italy with coal and her place was taken by Germany.[47] Although Mussolini had spoken of conquering an empire and then returning in strength to the Brenner before Germany had rearmed, Italian acquiescence in the German-Austrian agreement of July 1936 was clearly a first step towards an Anschluss which would be unopposed by Rome. Collaboration on Franco's side in the Spanish civil war led to the announcement of the Axis in November 1936. As Mussolini's contempt for the western democracies grew 'the brutal friendship', with its advantages and dangers, became an inescapable reality.

The easy successes of the Ethiopian campaign, which had raised Mussolini and Badoglio to the pinnacle of their popularity in Italy, made it very difficult for those soldiers and civilians who saw dangers ahead and sought a critical appraisal of Italy's war potential. Many of the junior officers had been attracted by the ideas of Douhet, but Badoglio dismissed him as a madman and an ex-convict. General Grazioli's pleas for motorisation of the army and close air support fell on deaf ears. The general staff closed all the military journals to him and he only obtained a hearing by writing for *Nuova Antologia*. Likewise, his enthusiastic report on the unconventional tactics employed during the Soviet manoeuvres in the Ukraine were ignored by the general staff, who deplored such 'false heresies'.[48] When asked whether the Italian navy should build aircraft carriers, the Duce replied that this was unnecessary as Italy herself was one gigantic aircraft carrier. When anyone questioned the efficiency of the air force, or queried the figures, or wondered whether winning cups in transatlantic air races was really an effective substitute for a fighting service with clear objectives, Mussolini would remind them that his air force could blot out the sun.

The general staff described Mussolini as a military genius, a *condot-*

tiero 'who prepared, led, and won the greatest colonial victory in modern history'.[49] First World War soldier number 12467 became, with the king, the first Marshal of the Empire. As the regime never tired of pointing out, the Duce was always right, and it was the duty of every Italian 'to believe, to obey, and to fight'. Minculpop (the ministry of popular culture), with the connivance of the military hierarchy, convinced the majority of Italians, and many beyond the Alps, of the invincibility of the armed forces. There was much talk of '*otto milioni di baionetti*', of a nation in arms with its '*figli della lupa*' and '*balila moschetieri*.'

When Mussolini visited Germany in 1937 he was impressed and at the same time depressed by the military and industrial might of the Reich. He knew he could not match German strength, could not afford to be ranged against her and yet if he became a close ally Italy would become very much a junior partner. The Germans were always politely sceptical of Mussolini's claims, and this made him unwilling to engage in joint military planning as it would expose the weaknesses of his system. Nevertheless, Italy joined the Anti-Comintern pact on 6 November 1937 and, after considerable delay, signed the Pact of Steel with Germany on 22 May 1939. Inexorably, despite Ciano's growing reluctance and Mussolini's vacillation, Italy was being strapped to the German war chariot.

In March 1938 in a speech to the senate, Mussolini declared:

> We aim to prepare men and means for a lightning war (*guerra di rapido corso*) . . . In fascist Italy the problem of unified command which torments other countries is resolved. Politico-strategic objectives of war are drawn up by the Head of Government. Their implementation is entrusted to the chief of general staff . . . History shows — including our own — that division between the political and military conduct of war was always fatal . . . In Italy the war, as it was in Africa, will be directed under the orders of the king, by one man: the man who now speaks to you.[50]

It has already been indicated that this reference to streamlined efficiency was a façade.

General Favagrossa, who replaced the veteran Dallolio as commisary general for war production at the end of August 1939, swiftly divined this world of illusion where staff officers played a complicated numbers game to which Badoglio was rarely invited. In 1938, for example, he had not been informed of the decision to reduce the number of regiments in a division from three to two, thus producing the notorious 'hollow legions'. Favagrossa learnt that another decision, to replace Italy's vintage guns with modern artillery — a move which Dallolio had advocated since the 1920s — arose as a result of the Duce overhearing the adverse comments of German officers at a military parade.[51] Favagrossa realised that the situation was equally serious with regard to tanks and motorisation. The military hierarchy had ignored the lessons of the Spanish civil war,[52] and the German manoeuvres. They had assured the Duce that Italy's frontiers were unsuitable for tank warfare.

It was apparent, therefore, that a lightning war, despite the bombastic speeches, was out of the question. The army possessed 1,500 tanks but only 70 were medium; the rest were three-ton machines which the troops dismissed as 'sardine tins'.[53] There was a desperate shortage of lorries, armoured cars and other vehicles, but even in basic commodities like uniforms Favagrossa found that 15 out of the 67 divisions (73 in 1940) were deficient, that the infantry were equipped with rifles of the 1891 model if they were equipped at all. The air force possessed 2,500 machines (3,400 in 1940), but there were dozens of different types, the fighters were too slow and armament and armour too weak. Radio equipment was poor and there was only sufficient aviation fuel for four months. The navy also had similar problems, but what most alarmed Favagrossa was the inability of Italy's war industries to supply the armed forces.

On 1 March 1937 the Fascist Grand Council had called for a massive autarkic drive but the money and the organisation were missing. The three armed services continued to compete with one another for military equipment, while Italy's financial troubles necessitated the continued export of such equipment right up to June 1940. In 1939 the army asked for 15,000 guns but Italian industry could produce only 700. In aircraft production the factories could turn out 150 aircraft per month, but under the stimulus of war this rose to 300 by 1942, when it was already too late.[54] On every level there was lack of co-ordination, and Favagrossa pointed this out to the Duce and Badoglio. Italy needed five to ten years to reorganise and prepare for a major war. If Italy became involved in war before then she would have to rely on two things: Mussolini's genius for bluff and German support. In the event, the first failed and the second prolonged the death agony.

What made a difficult situation virtually impossible was the Duce's failure to decide on precise objectives. Unless the general staff or those in charge of war production knew what plans were envisaged it was impossible for them to concentrate their energies. Bastianini noticed that Mussolini never really studied plans seriously because this entailed calculating risks and advantages and directing resources towards some specific goal.[55] He refused to define his expansionist aims or let Badoglio or the Germans define them for him. His attack on Albania in April 1939 seemed to owe as much to a desire to match Hitler's occupation of Prague as to a determination to pursue a coherent Balkan policy. The attack on France in June 1940 was a desperate last-minute effort which totally ignored the strategic or tactical problems involved. His Mediterranean war against Britain was based on the un-wise premise that she would surrender shortly after the collapse of France. Consequently, German suggestions that Italy concentrate on a drive into Egypt or the elimination of Malta went unheeded. The attack on Greece was a strategic, diplomatic and psychological blunder of the first magnitude and effectively ended Italy's credibility as a sig-nificant military power and her independence of action within the Axis.

Even if Mussolini had set about the task of dominating the Mediter-ranean more effectively he would have been almost fatally handicapped by the fact that the armed forces had never been encouraged to think in terms of combined operations. Many of the officers and men were in-sufficiently trained for conventional warfare. The 800,000 members of the militia could be written off as effective troops – and had been by the regulars for the past eighteen years. In 1940, that left a regular army of just over one and a half million (not the eight million bayonets of the propagandists). There were too many senior officers – in 1939 there were, for instance, 600 generals, one for every 33 officers – and too few trained junior officers, those of the reserve being particularly ill equipped to lead men into battle. There were only two NCOs per company compared with twenty in the German Army.[56] If Hitler had complied with Mussolini's extravagant demands on 26 August 1939 and sent the raw materials and weapons demanded, Italian industry would have been unable to cope and the armed forces would have been unable to use them effectively.

In his war diary, General Armellini noted that from 1933 the general staff gradually lost all initiative in technical affairs and virtually ceased to function, 'Politics remained uncontested master of the field; *il bluff* which already dominated political, economic, financial and cultural developments in the nation also permeated the military sphere.'[57] When the general staff met to compile lists of urgent needs on 18 November 1939 their deliberations were interrupted by chief of air staff Pricolo who pointed out that as the three different services were using different methods of computation their final figures would be meaningless.[58] On a more heroic note, in June 1940 Marshal Balbo was shot down over Tobruk by his own artillery. This dashing commander-in-chief for North Africa, former quadrumvir, former head of the air force who in many ways was a representative exemplar of the fascist style, was killed after leaping into an aircraft to pursue the ever-elusive British armoured cars just a few hours after forbidding his subordinates to over-react in this manner.[59]

The tragic results of Mussolini's policies, of the failure of Badoglio and the staff officers to insist upon reforms and resign if this was denied, of the general unpreparedness of the armed forces and Italy to fight a serious war, is perhaps best described by a veteran of the Greek war. He spoke of the troops who did their duty 'although they had a thousand excellent reasons for not doing it, while their leaders blundered from the beginning to the end of a campaign outstanding in Italian history as an example of political improvidence, military incompetence, petty ambition and strategic and tactical shortsightedness.'[60]

While the Italian forces were suffering 100,000 casualties in Greece, and tens of thousands were being killed or about to be killed on the Russian front or in North Africa, the Duce, a political journalist of genius but no war lord, was enhancing his growing reputation for producing a skilful blend of tragedy and farce. He was ordering a concentration of blackshirts on bicycles in Bologna for a blitzkrieg on Ljubljana. Or was it to reinforce the Brenner against a German attempt to absorb the Alto Adige? Or was it merely to provide a newspaper headline to illustrate fascist dynamism? Perhaps — and this is the most damning of all — perhaps he didn't know and didn't care. On the road to Salo and the Piazzale San Loreto he had time to recollect and reconsider, but all he published was an apologia.[61]

Notes

1. E. von Rintelen, *Mussolini l'alleato*, Rome, 1952, p. 108.
2. H.R. Trevor-Roper (ed.), *Hitler's War Directives 1939-45*, London, 1973, pp. 98-100.
3. The article and Badoglio's supposed reply can be found in G. Bianchi, *Perche e come cadde il fascismo*, Milan, 1970, pp. 206-9.
4. G. Bocca, *Storia d'Italia nella guerra fascista*, Bari, 1969, p. 291.
5. G. Ciano, *Ciano's diary 1939-1943*, London, 1974, pp. 309-10.
6. P. Pieri and G. Rochat, *Badoglio*, Turin, 1974, p. 767. The period after 1918 is the sole responsibility of Rochat.
7. This was the view of ex-minister for African affairs Alessandro Lessona in

his *Memorie,* Florence, 1958, pp. 401-2.
8.   G. Rochat, 'L'esercito e il fascismo', G. Quazza (ed.), *Fascismo e societa italiana,* Turin, 1973, p. 103.
9.   D. Mack Smith, *Mussolini's Roman Empire,* London, 1976.
10. Ciano, p. 321.
11. Ibid., p. 328.
12. E. Rossi, *Mussolini e lo stato maggiore,* Rome, 1951, p. 15.
13. B. Mussolini, *Storia di un anno,* Verona, 1944.
14. C. de Biase, *L'Aquila d'oro,* Milan, 1970, pp. 409, 412, L. Federzoni, *Italia di ieri per la storia di domani,* Milan, 1967, p. 189.
15. Bianchi, p. 69. M. Toscano, *The Origins of the Pact of Steel,* Baltimore, 1967, p. 226.
16. Biase, p. 401.
17. Watt, pp. 116-17.
18. Ciano, 18 September 1939, p. 155.
19. Rochat, p. 108.
20. Watt, p. 142.
21. Ciano, 12 October 1940, p. 297.
22. S. Visconti Prasca, *Io ho aggredite la Grecia,* Rome, 1946, p. 46.
23. Ciano, 17 October 1940, p. 298.
24. Ibid., 18 October 1940, pp. 298-9.
25. Pieri and Rochat, pp. 763-4. Also in agreement with this interpretation are M. Cervi, *The Hollow Legions,* London, 1972, and C. Cruikshank, *Greece 1940-41,* London, 1976.
26. Pieri and Rochat, p. 758.
27. M. Cervi, p. 70.
28. G. Rochat, 'Mussolini et les forces armées', Comité d'histoire de la 2e guerre mondiale, *La Guerre en Méditerranée 1939-45,* Paris,1971, p. 39.
29. G. Sabbatucci, *I combattenti nel primo depoguerra,* Bari, 1974,pp. 14-19.
30. M. Isnenghi, *Il mito della grande guerra,* Bari, 1970, pp. 306-8, and A. Serpieri, *Le guerra e le classi rurali italiane,* Bari, 1930, pp. 41-2, 49, 68.
31. For this and Badoglio's equivocal attitude see Pieri and Rochat, pp. 511-14.
32. G. Rochat, *L'Esercito italiano da Vittorio Veneto a Mussolini,* Bari, 1967, p. 502.
33. Ibid., pp. 530-1.
34. Ibid., pp. 226-7, 518.
35. Ibid., p. 519.
36. Watt, p. 43.
37. Pieri and Rochat, p. 566.
38. Ibid., p. 559.
39. Ibid., p. 556
40. Rochat, *L'Esercito,* p. 568.
41. Pieri and Rochat, pp. 569-72.
42. Ibid., pp. 748-9.
43. Bianchi, p. 11.
44. Rossi, p. 166.
45. R. Guariglia, *Ricordi: 1922-1946,* Naples, 1950, p. 146. For a discussion of the diplomats see H. Stuart Hughes, 'The early diplomacy of Italian fascism', and F. Gilbert, 'Ciano and his ambassadors', in G. Craig and F. Gilbert (eds.), *The Diplomats,* Princeton, 1953.
46. R. Sarti, *The ax within,* New York, 1974, p. 11.
47. E. Wiskemann, *The Rome Berlin Axis,* rev. edn., London, 1966, p. 76.
48. Biase, pp. 380-5.
49. Ibid., p. 403.

50. Bianchi, p. 13.
51. C. Favagrossa, *Perche perdemmo la guerra,* Milan, 1946, p. 13.
52. The best recent account is J. Coverdale, *Italian Intervention in the Spanish Civil War,* Princeton, 1975.
53. Favagrossa, p. 16.
54. Ibid., pp. 19-24. Bocca, p. 52.
55. G. Bastianini, *Uomini, cose, fatti,* Milan, 1959, p. 42. 'When he ventured to suggest that Italy was unprepared for war, the Duce roared that that implied that he had done nothing for 18 years. Attolico, feeling faint, had to retire for a glass of water and when he returned they spoke of coal deliveries – in other words, the indirect approach' (ibid., pp. 62-3).
56. Bocca, p. 103.
57. Q. Armellini, *Diario di guerra,* Milan, 1946, pp. 292-3.
58. Biase, p. 431.
59. Bocca, p. 214.
60. Cervi, p. x.
61. E. Faldella, *L'Italia nella 2a guerra mondiale,* Bologna, 1959, p. 16.

6 'THE UNNECESSARY WAR'? MILITARY ADVICE AND FOREIGN POLICY IN GREAT BRITAIN, 1931-1939

David Dilks

How comely it is and how reviving to a British historian to learn, after all these years, that the policy pursued by the governments of Mac-Donald, Baldwin and Chamberlain between 1931 and 1939 was not uniquely foolish, shortsighted, ineffective, not merely a catalogue of wrong measurements and feeble impulses, whereby insular and deluded simpletons led a great power from a position of ample strength to one of humiliating defeat. Pondering upon all that we have been told about the military preparations and the foreign policies pursued in the same period by Germany and Russia and Italy, we may with profit examine afresh the record of British governments in the 1930s; we may even discover that they understood the essential nature of the problems with which they were confronted in strategy and foreign policy, and that they made intelligent, though in some respects admittedly ineffective, efforts to minimise and meet them. Indeed, the account of 'planning' in the Fascist dictatorship, dedicated to belief, obedience and struggle, reminded me of the occasion at a grim time of the Second World War when Mr Churchill gazed at his handful of colleagues in the embattled Cabinet Room and said, 'You know, this isn't such a bad government after all.' No one said much in response. After a little pause the Prime Minister went a stage further: 'I think it is quite a good government.' After a further pause, he announced with a beaming smile, 'Indeed, when I reflect soberly upon the matter, I cannot in a political lifetime of more than forty years recall a government which has so completely commanded my confidence.'

We are accustomed to be told that in the nineteenth century, Great Britain 'ruled the world'; that she imposed by the exercise of naval strength a 'Pax Britannica'; that she existed, at least in the latter part of the century, in a state of 'splendid isolation', able to intervene or to abstain from conflict at will, detached from the need to join entangling alliances and to pay the price for them. This conception, in the hands of imaginative writers, is used to render more startling the contrast with the failures and fumblings of the 1930s. Yet the Royal Navy of the nineteenth century was not always stronger than its likely opponents in combination; that century was in fact characterised by an abundance of wars, in some of which the British were involved and others of which they were powerless to prevent; and the ministers who had to operate the policy would have said that the isolation was often more notable than the splendour. In those issues which could be decided by the exercise of sea power the British commonly, though not always, prevailed. In questions likely to be determined by the exercise of land power, the British frequently found themselves impotent. Thus the old Prime Minister Lord Salisbury, urged to intervene in the Armenian massacres, politely lamented his inability to place the Royal Navy upon the slopes of Mount Ararat, rather as Mr Chamberlain regretted that he could not deploy capital ships amidst the hills of Bohemia.

Britain's retention and extension of a great empire in the late nineteenth century rested upon three conditions: first, that potential opponents should mistrust each other more than they disliked the British; secondly, that the British Empire should not save in North America share a land frontier with a first-class power; and thirdly, the enjoyment of luck. Salisbury had simultaneously presided over and regarded with unease the growth of British dominion, and therefore of British risks, in areas remote from the sea. As he used to remind his Cabinet and Parliament, he seemed to have heard of a place called Khartoum, and of an expedition to relieve the force of a certain General Gordon, the results of which had not been of the most brilliant character. The expenditure of the British Government upon the Army and the Royal Navy, though substantial, was by no means adequate in relation to the dangers; and there existed no machinery outside the Cabinet for bringing into focus or harmony the foreign policy of the British Empire and the capacity to defend its interests.

During the worst phase of the Boer War, there was not a single complete battalion left in the British Isles. In the famous phrase, the British had had 'no end of a lesson'. More prosaically, Balfour, who succeeded his uncle as Prime Minister in 1902, remarked, 'Our usual luck has held again.' By then, the British had at least taken some steps to limit their liabilities.

The rise of a great indigenous power in the Far East meant either that Britain must be content to exist upon Japan's sufferance, or that she must increase her own naval strength in eastern waters, or that she should seek to ally with Japan. When the alliance was announced, even the Emperor William II (who used to solace himself by commenting tartly upon the incapacity of British ministers) observed, 'The noodles

have had a lucid interval.' The alliance strengthened Britain's hand
against Russia, not to mention Japan's ability to try conclusions with
Russia. It gave France more incentive to make her peace with Britain.
The identification of Germany as a potentially great naval power, and
therefore rival; the burying of feuds with France and Russia; the establishment of the Committee of Imperial Defence, of which the Prime
Minister was the only permanent member and which brought together
the politicians and representatives of the War Office and Admiralty, but
not of the Foreign Office; the reform of the Army under Haldane; all
these steps indicated a serious effort to achieve some concordance
between foreign policy and military capacity.

The first concern of every British government remained the defence
of the Empire and of the sea routes which sustained it; Parliament
accepted the principle that the Royal Navy must remain superior to its
likely enemies. Moreover, the British Isles were declared in those days,
before the invention of aviation, to be secure from serious invasion. And
yet in 1914 and after the policy of reliance upon a supreme Navy was
shown to be inadequate. The land force which the British could despatch at once to Europe, though brave, well-trained and well-equipped,
was tiny. The British Government had felt to the last that it could not
promise a firm commitment to France. It is true that eventually Great
Britain emerged from the war victorious; but only by improvising enormous armies, by cashing in assets acquired during decades of prosperity,
and then by borrowing on her allies' account. As for that great mass of
British possessions east of Suez, they had suffered no serious harm. The
First World War had in practice been confined largely to Europe and
the Middle East, the Atlantic and the North Sea; after Christmas of
1914, Britain did not deploy a single capital ship east of Suez.

Many of those problems which had preoccupied successive British
governments before the First World War continued to dominate the
minds of their successors. Naturally enough, the proportions changed
somewhat; for instance, the prospect of a serious Russian threat to
India or the buffer states, though not dismissed, occupied a less prominent place in the thinking of the interwar years than it had done before
1905. The defence of France and the Low Countries mattered more,
partly because the events of 1914 and after had shown that Britain
could not afford a French defeat, and partly because the development
of military aviation meant that Britain had in some senses ceased to be
an island. By the Locarno treaties of 1925, Britain did what she had
refused to do before 1914 in pledging herself to the defence of certain
frontiers in western Europe. The first claim on the attention of British

governments however, remained the defence of the British Empire, which had emerged enlarged, rather than strengthened, in 1919. Some of the newly acquired territories added little to Britain's liabilities; others, of which the best example is Palestine, added a great deal. Indeed, in the years 1936 to 1939 Palestine consistently absorbed more British troops than were available for despatch to Europe.

This sprawl of territories, some independent, some proceeding towards independence, some wholly dependent; of trading interests and protectorates; of investments and routes without which British trade could not flow, British troops move, British exports earn enough currency to keep the country alive; all this constituted a serious but manageable obligation in relatively peaceful times, and an impossible burden if the potential enemies could not be kept apart. That was the essential difference between the period from 1934 to 1939, the five years from the collapse of the Disarmament Conference to the invasion of Poland, and the quinquennium from, say, the outbreak of the Boer War to the conclusion of the Anglo-French agreement of 1904. Four partner countries of the Empire had for practical purposes become independent. It was and is convenient simply to call them 'the Dominions', though their attitudes, perceptions of threats and lack of threats, likely involvement in war, geographical position, varied widely. They were not committed to Britain's foreign policy, nor would they any longer be automatically at war upon the King's declaration, as they had been in 1914; on the other hand, they made precious little provision for their own defence.

To put the problem in simple terms, an island lying off the shores of Europe, deficient in all the main minerals except coal, unable to grow more than about half its food and with a population of rather more than 40 million, was supposed to defend territories in every continent except Europe, covering in total about a quarter of the habitable surface of the globe and including about a quarter of its population. Doubtless it exaggerates somewhat to express the dilemma in terms so stark; for example, it was not likely that Canada would be attacked by another power, and if she were so attacked, she would in all probability be defended by the United States. In theory the United States herself might be the aggressor; in which event there would be precious little that the British could do about it. All the same, there is no possibility of understanding the British dilemma between the wars, of measuring the gap separating planning and foreign policy between 1931 and 1939, or of judging fairly the statesmen of those times, unless this central and cardinal fact is grasped; it was the attempt to meet threats in widely separated theatres, in the first instance from Japan and then Germany and later from Italy, that imposed acute strains, and often a condition approaching paralysis, on British foreign policy.

Clearly Britain could not detach herself from all concern with events in Europe; nor could she regard this or that country of the British Empire as expendable. British interests in south-east Asia and in the Far East were too great to be treated as extremities which in the last resort, however painful the process, some enemy might be allowed to hack off. So large an aggregation of territories and lives could be held only if the British sustained what they called for conversational shorthand their prestige, by which they meant the reputation for invincibility. The possession of Empire, in short, was of greater significance to the international position of Britain than, say, to France.

Most of the powers whom the British faced as potential enemies in the 1930s had, by contrast, comparatively compact interests; German interests were concentrated in Europe, the North Sea and eventually in other waters; Italy's in central, south-eastern and southern Europe, the Mediterranean, the Middle East and East Africa; Japan's in the western Pacific and in Manchuria and China. Those three powers were united by little in the way of common interests, but the possession of a common potential enemy will make up for many little local differences, and the British filled the role admirably.

In one of Conan Doyle's stories, Holmes draws the attention of the inspector to the curious incident of the dog in the night. Said the inspector, 'The dog did nothing in the night-time.' 'That', Holmes retorted, 'was the curious incident.' Although it would be positively un-neighbourly to suggest that the United States 'did nothing' in the international politics of the interwar period, it is none the less true that the part played by the two great powers at the periphery, America and Russia, was far less than their involvement in the First World War, their actual or latent strength, their territory and resources, would have warranted. It is at least arguable that a deeper engagement — not because it was a duty of the United States or Russia to protect the interests of other states, but because both so manifestly failed in the end to protect their own interests — would have saved at least one of them the terrible price paid in 1941 and after. There is of course a plausible reason for the extreme caution displayed by the British and the Russians alike; both were balancing, especially after 1937, the risk of war in the Far East against the risk of war in Europe.

The burdens which the British and French were supposed to shoulder, tolerable as they seemed in the 1920s when the central powers and Turkey had collapsed, proved in the end disproportionate to their strength. Obligations which Britain undertook towards France, Belgium and Germany by the Locarno agreements of 1925 were intended to reassure the French, to induce a more gentle treatment of Germany, and to demonstrate to Stresemann and his colleagues that Germany would obtain more by co-operation with the West than she could ever get from alignment with Russia. The British had disarmed effectively and with promptitude after the war. They had ceased to make any provision for intervention on the mainland of Europe. As the Chiefs of Staff explained to the Cabinet after the Locarno agreements, the modest expeditionary force and a very limited number of squadrons constituted the only military instrument which the British could use in Europe, but were available only when the requirements of imperial defence permitted. It would be hard to imagine a simpler and clearer statement of the primacy of imperial commitments.

That state of affairs was accepted by successive Cabinets, reminded from time to time by the Chiefs of Staff that they had received neither instructions nor resources to build up forces which would enable Britain to honour the Locarno commitment. In the circumstances of the late 1920s, this mattered comparatively little, since Germany was incapable of attacking France and Belgium, and after the unhappy experiences in the Ruhr of 1923 and 1924 it was not likely that France and Belgium would attack Germany. Now, no one supposes that the foreign policy of the British Empire could simply be founded upon military advice. Successive governments had to weigh their own esti-mates of political possibilities and financial opportunities against the other risks, and the slaughter during the First World War produced two effects of particular seriousness in the formulation of British foreign policy: a dread of possible repetition, with a conviction that Britain should never again put Kitchener armies into the field in Europe; and a feeling of relaxation, since the likely enemies were defeated. Or so it seemed; for after all everything turned on the definition of likely enemies.

Perhaps there was during this period no more ominous change in Britain's international position than the loss of the Anglo-Japanese alliance and its conversion first into neutrality and eventually into open enmity. By the Washington agreements of 1921-2 naval primacy in home waters had been deliberately conferred upon Japan. The ratios agreed for capital ships meant that Britain could deploy greater strength in Far Eastern waters than could Japan, even without the active support of the United States; but only if there were secure lines of communication, a base capable of sustaining and fuelling a great fleet, and an absence of serious threat elsewhere. Even Churchill, who was apt to take on the colour of his surroundings, dismissed during his time as Chancellor of the Exchequer any thought of war with Japan. He urged that the military estimates must be contained or cut down, pointing out that the Government would be giving political hostages to fortune if it allowed itself to spend too little on social services and too much on arms.

The service departments had been instructed since 1919 to work on the rule that the British Empire would not be engaged in a major war for ten years, and before Baldwin's second government left office, the ten-year rule had been placed on a new basis, whereby it was to roll forward until countermanded. The construction of the vast base at Singapore, until the completion of which Britain had no base east of Malta capable of refitting a capital ship, was several times initiated and suspended. Not until 1938 was it completed, and even then Singapore lacked essential defences; but by that time the situation in the Mediterranean, the Middle East and Europe had become so threatening that the British never dared to place in the Far East the eight or nine capital ships which the Admiralty would in easier circumstances have wished to send.

There is no denying that a substantial chasm already separated Britain's commitments from her ability to fulfil them. The Cabinet had failed to discern the imminence of the threat in the Far East. Even as late as 1930, at the time of the London Naval Conference, Ramsay MacDonald felt able to override the earnest advice of the Admiralty and settle for fifty cruisers rather than the seventy which the sailors declared to be the irreducible minimum. Moreover, the provisions of the London Naval Treaty did not apply to France or Italy. The Treaty extended the holiday in the building of capital ships until the end of 1936, an issue of particular import to the British because most of their battleships were obsolescent. Very soon the collapse of international credit, the rise in unemployment, the disintegration of the Labour Government, the abandonment of the gold standard and the return of a National Government pledged to a balancing of the budget and the restoration of financial confidence, would deflect attention from the dangers abroad. The economic storm, coupled with the opening of the disarmament conference, made the Cabinet more reluctant than ever to spend on defence the large sums required by any realistic view of British prospects.

It is seductive and convenient for historians to discover turning

points. Nevertheless, and seeing how narrow was the margin of survival
in 1940, the events at Shanghai early in 1932 may be taken to mark
such a point. The crisis in the Far East, beginning with Japan's seizure
of Manchuria, showed how hollow were the assumptions of the ten-
year rule. When it is remembered that defence planning was still proceeding on the assumption that the British Empire would not be engaged in a major war at least until 1942, the plain fact that the British
bases east of Suez would be useless against a determined Japan could
not fail to be alarming to any minister, no matter how earnestly he
might long for the reduction of unemployment, the return of solvency
or the reign of international peace. Although it took some little time
before the ten-year rule was officially scrapped, and, more importantly,
before the Chancellor of the Exchequer felt that he could finance a
large programme of rearmament, the fact that the Japense had not been
deterred from attacking an area where British interests were directly at
stake probably did more to awaken the British Government than the
mere fact of Japanese expansion in areas with which Britain was less
directly concerned. The Foreign Secretary of the day, Sir John Simon,
felt no more confidence than any other Prime Minister or Foreign
Secretary of the interwar period that American goodwill would be
translated into an economic or military policy which would give Japan
serious pause; nor has any evidence emerging from the American
archives since those days indicated that the conviction was ill-founded.

Of course, there is another gulf to be noticed, a clear view of which
had been occluded by the circumstances of the 1920s. On a strict
reading of the Covenant, to the upholding of which all parties in Britain
had proclaimed their devotion, the integrity of member states was to be
defended, by moral pressure, by economic sanctions or in the last resort
by military force. An attack upon a remote area – for instance, Manchuria or Abyssinia – should on this view have been opposed as vigorously as an attack upon some neighbouring state or vital possession.
These were ambitious and sweeping obligations, the cause of disquiet
from the outset and not least to the government of Canada. They had
been first written into the Covenant when it had been confidently
expected that all great powers would be members, and devoted members at that, of the League. That membership was never achieved; the
obligations, in theory at any rate, remained.

The Chiefs of Staff were entirely justified in pointing out that the
ten-year rule had no warrant in history or in the observed facts. Moreover, it had no counterpart in any foreign country and had produced in
the Far East a situation wherein, before the arrival of a British battle

fleet (always assuming that there was a base from which it could operate), Japan might have captured the facilities and fuel supplies on which
the ships would depend for the final stages of their passage and for
mobility after arrival. It would be the height of folly, they advised, to
perpetuate Britain's defenceless state there.[1]

The manifest failure of the Disarmament Conference, long-drawn
though the agony proved to be, the breakdown of the revised arrangements for reparations, the mounting disorders in Germany and the
installation of Hitler in power at the end of January 1933 all gave point
to these warnings. The Permanent Under-Secretary of the Foreign
Office, Sir Robert Vansittart, never doubted that Hitler's regime meant
to pursue a policy of rearmament until Germany was once more a
threatening military power. Since Japan was heavily armed and
Germany was not, the Chiefs of Staff at that stage regarded the Far East
as taking a higher priority than European commitments, with the
defence of India running third. Work upon the Singapore base was
accelerated from the spring of 1933. The Chancellor became a little less
reluctant during that year, as the economic situation slowly improved,
to contemplate extra spending on defence, though neither he nor his
leading colleagues in the Cabinet had yet any conception of the sums
which they would be disbursing within a few years for that purpose.

It was the rise of Germany as a potentially great power that now
began to give British defence planning a new shape and seriousness.
With so many accumulated deficiencies, such grievous economic
problems and such daunting political difficulties at home, how was the
situation to be faced? The Chiefs of Staff had only just declared that
for the moment Britain was not capable of defeating Japan. What was
to happen if, at the opposite end of the world, Germany became a great
military force again? As Mr Churchill used to remark, no one who had
been at death grips with the German war machine wished to repeat the
experience. Worse still, what would happen if Germany and Japan came
together to exploit these weaknesses?[2] The British Government never
considered seriously a policy of preventing Germany from rearmament
by the exercise of physical force; that is, by the threat to place a British
or French army in Germany unless rearmament ceased. In *The
Gathering Storm*, Churchill argues that this should have been done, and
writes, as he used to speak at the time, about the folly of disarming
before the grievances of the vanquished had been met, and about the
physical security enjoyed by the victorious allies.

What is less clear is how these physical securities were to be used.
There was no longer an army in occupation of any part of German

territory, for it had been withdrawn in 1930, five years ahead of the
date laid down by the Versailles Treaty. Had a part of that army
remained in Germany, it might have been possible to use Germany's
manifest rearmament as a reason for retaining it there or strengthening
it. All this, however, dwells in the realms of theory. As French
ministers put it to Mr Eden in 1934, they were not thinking of a preventive war; still less was anybody in England doing so. The British
therefore already found themselves in a dilemma from which they
never succeeded in escaping; they could neither disinterest themselves
in Europe nor commit themselves there wholeheartedly. Embroilment
in a European struggle might well provide Japan with an opportunity
for a more determined assault upon British interests; conversely, war
with Japan might easily increase Germany's power for mischief in
Europe, or even render the British Isles liable to devastating attack
from the air and eventually to invasion.

All this was apprehended before the troubles with Italy over
Abyssinia in 1935-6, or the addition of Italy to the list of possible
enemies. It is conceivable, but no more, that a bold policy of rearmament, largely concentrated upon Europe, would have enabled additional guarantees of security to be offered to France, and Germany to
be contained. Whether even the most determined political leadership
could have enabled such a policy to be put immediately into effect at
the end of 1933, when the Disarmament Conference was still sitting
and the tide of pacific feeling running at its highest, remains a matter
for speculation.

Ministers were not presented with an agreed strategic doctrine by
their Service advisers. The more vigorous advocates of air power con-
tended that its development might soon make the capital ship a liability. Furthermore, it was argued that concentrated bombardment
from the air might terrorise civilians, destroy communications, sewerage
and transport in great cities, and disrupt industrial production on such a
scale that peace might have to be sought. The attention of the
Admiralty was mainly directed to the Far East, since Germany had not
yet begun to rebuild her navy. The main duty of the exiguous army
still lay in the defence of India and other imperial possessions, with the
possibility of despatching an expeditionary force to Europe to sustain
allies there, whereas the thinking of the Air Staff concentrated chiefly
upon the dangers in Europe.

The Committee of Imperial Defence, and the established machinery
of British Government, provided no easy method of reconciling the
conflicting claims. Long past were the days when the Prime Minister

himself could preside at every meeting of the CID and interest himself
in the details of its work. The machinery of the CID, spawning numerous sub-committees, was too cumbrous and slow-moving for the
swift resolution of issues so momentous. Its presiding spirit, also Secretary to the Cabinet, was Sir Maurice Hankey; a figure of legendary
efficiency and influence, dedicated to the upholding of British naval
strength, at the hub of affairs since 1912, and virtual creator of the
Cabinet Office. There was no ministry of supply and no minister of
defence in the modern sense, though the post of minister for the co-
ordination of defence was created in 1936. There was no effective
forum, outside the intermittent imperial conferences, in which the full
range of issues could be thrashed out with representatives of the
Dominions. No body could argue on anything like equal terms with the
Treasury about the economic consequences of a war. Ministerial
committees had sometimes advised the Cabinet about large questions
of foreign policy, or about particular crises.

The situation revealed by the autumn of 1933, however, was so
alarming that new expedients were called for. It is to be remembered
that the Prime Minister, MacDonald, was nearing the end of his political
life and unwell; the Lord President of the Council, Baldwin, commanded the parliamentary cohorts but lapsed easily into indecision and
was only fitfully effective. The position of the Chancellor of the Exchequer in a government committed to retrenchment and economy was
certain to be a strong one, and the more so in these circumstances.
Among ministers, Neville Chamberlain was the strongest single force in
the shaping of British defence policy between 1934 and 1939. This is
not to say that he always had his way.

On Chamberlain's proposal, France, the United States and Italy
were excluded as powers against whom Britain should make defensive
preparations; and a committee was established to prepare a programme
which would meet the worst deficiencies. Very few, and certainly not
the Chancellor of the Exchequer, realised how heroic a task this was to
prove. Nevertheless, this signals the end of the phase in which the financial risks were considered to outweigh the admittedly serious military
risks. The Chiefs-of-Staff, together with the Permanent Under-
Secretaries of the Treasury and the Foreign Office, were to meet under
the chairmanship of Sir Maurice Hankey to prepare a programme which
would meet the worst deficiencies. The deliberations of this powerful
group, and of the ministerial committee which considered its first
report, mark the inauguration of the effort to measure prospective as
well as actual weaknesses in the British Empire's defensive position, and

to recommend ways in which foreign policy could be so conducted as to minimise the risks. The first report of the Defence Requirements Committee (DRC) shows a tilting of the balance from the Far East towards Europe, a jerky, hesitant but inexorable process which did not reach completion until the decisions of 1939 to create a continental army, to give guarantees in eastern and south-eastern Europe and to introduce conscription. True, the DRC identified Japan as the most important immediate enemy. Germany, however, was identified as the ultimate potential enemy against whom Britain's defence policy must be directed in the longer term, and essentially for a simple reason: though the British Empire might suffer the severing of an artery or the loss of a limb in south-east Asia or the Far East, it was only from Europe that the heart of the Empire could be pierced.

Hankey and his colleagues proposed a programme of spending spread over five years. It would cost an additional £70 million. Ironically enough, this report eventually ended with the ministerial committee on disarmament. The identification of Germany as the ultimate potential enemy owed much to the unrelenting advocacy of Sir Robert Vansittart and Sir Warren Fisher.[3] Hankey, with his attention focused upon the naval defence of the British Empire, was at one with the Chief of the Imperial General Staff in doubting whether Germany could be ready for war in five years.

On the other hand, and ironically in view of so much that has been said and written in the last forty years, it was Chamberlain who of all the senior ministers most clearly identified Germany as the enemy against whom the main British effort must be concentrated. Chamberlain — or perhaps it would be more accurate to say Chamberlain, Fisher and senior officials of the Treasury — had come to the conclusion that uncertainty in British defence policy had continued long enough, and that since Britain's resources were not unlimited, and since she seemed unlikely to acquire allies stronger than France, there must be some cutting of the coat according to the cloth. As Chamberlain remarked pithily, 'We cannot provide simultaneously for hostilities with Japan and Germany.'[4] He recorded on a number of occasions during 1934 that the quarter from which a challenge to Britain's safety might materialise was plainly Germany; hence the enthusiasm with which he seized on the recommendation of the DRC report that Britain should make a real effort to reach closer terms with Japan.

The events of 1934 — open German rearmament, the collapse of the Disarmament Conference, the murder of Dollfuss — gave point to this recommendation but perhaps encouraged Ministers to follow only part of the prescription; for it had been integral to the argument of the DRC that better relations with Japan could be attained only if Britain showed strength in the Far East and continued to do. Chamberlain strongly pressed the Foreign Secretary to respond to overtures recently made by Japan, and was more sanguine than the Far Eastern Department of the Foreign Office about the possibilities of reaching a better understanding. The policy proved abortive, and Chamberlain quickly recognised the fact; the interest of his proposals in this context lies in the clear recognition of Germany as the main enemy, and the determination to enforce some priorities as the only alternative to a helpless drift in defence and foreign policy alike.

The impression left by the minutes of the Defence Requirements Committee and the Chiefs of Staff Sub-Committee, and by many other documents, is not altogether reassuring about the quality of advice tendered at the highest levels by the Service Departments. The Secretary of State for Air, Lord Londonderry, much maligned then and later, had little political weight and had become a liability to the government. As for the Chief of the Air Staff, Chamberlain recorded, 'Ellington makes all of us despair.'[5]

Since there was agreement neither among the politicians nor among the fighting men about the true role of the British army, and since it had become a custom to treat the army even worse than the other services, the Secretaryship of State for War had long been regarded as a graveyard for politicians, and the War Office itself as something of a mild joke. (There is a celebrated story about a young officer from Canada who was sent to London in the winter of 1939 and ordered to report to the War Office. All the nameplates had been removed from the buildings, and to him all those great structures along Whitehall looked alike. He could not find the War Office. Salvation seemed to be at hand, however, when a smart naval officer came striding up the street. 'Excuse me, sir,' said the Canadian, 'can you tell me which side the War Office is on?' The Naval Officer thought for a while before replying, 'Well at the beginning of the war we thought they were on our side, but now we aren't sure.') There is nothing to suggest that the CIGS, Sir Archibald Montgomery-Massingberd, carried special weight.

The position of the Admiralty within the machine of government was a much stronger one; the First Lord, Sir Bilton Eyres-Monsell, had been a respected Chief Whip; and the First Sea Lord, Admiral Sir Ernle Chatfield, had charm, intelligence and decision. He was Chairman of the Chiefs of Staff Sub-Committee, and widely regarded as the brains of that body. It is a measure of the strength of the Admiralty on the one side, and of the Chancellor of the Exchequer on the other, that neither wholly won the day in the aftermath of the DRC's report.

Chamberlain argued that the chief danger to the British Isles lay in the air. Whatever else may be said of his approach, it was certainly not a conventional one; no minister was more willing than he, it appears, to throw away any number of fly-blown phylacteries, sometimes to the huge scandal of his colleagues. The requests of the Chief of the Air Staff had been so modest during the deliberations of the DRC that they were substantially increased in the outcome, chiefly at Chamberlain's instance.

Arguing from the premise that Britain could not afford to prepare against her two great potential opponents, Chamberlain at one point suggested measures which would for practical purposes have meant the abandonment of the Singapore strategy. The First Lord of the Admiralty said that this was a policy which not even the Communist Party advocated. The ubiquitous and influential Hankey took a stern line and told MacDonald and Baldwin that if the government were committed to any such policy, there would be no point in setting off for his impending tour of the Dominions, during which he was to explain British defence policy. Chamberlain, rather rarely for him, had to retreat somewhat and the practical consequences were less serious than they might otherwise have been, because the attempt to reach better terms with Japan soon failed and thereafter the Chancellor accepted that a substantial programme of naval expansion must be financed. In respect of cruisers and capital ships, Britain was in any case committed until the end of 1936 by the restrictions of the Washington and London Naval Treaties.

It would be pointless to make too much of the cuts which, again largely under Chamberlain's impetus, were made by the Cabinet in the total of spending recommended by the DRC. The fact was that the British capacity to manufacture sophisticated arms had been so seriously reduced that very large amounts could not be spent immediately; the first task would be to create the capacity. Within a short period, the reductions upon which the Chancellor had insisted were overtaken by the pressure of events and soon the Cabinet was spending sums undreamed of by the RAF or by anybody else when the first report of the DRC was drawn up. This observation applies especially to the air programmes; as for the British Expeditionary Force, the War Office was told that it must be reserved for the longer future and in practice the funds were not provided. As the cost of defence soared, the prospects of equipping an Expeditionary Force diminished; it was not until the winter after the Munich agreement that this order of priorities

reversed itself, and by then the financial arguments had more or less
ceased to apply.

In sum, Chamberlain, and perhaps to a lesser degree the other
members of the Cabinet, were attempting to take the logic of the DRC's
report to its conclusion; if Germany was determined upon rearmament,
had the basic resources of a great power and might launch into open
warfare within a few years, then Britain should bend every effort to
limit her liabilities elsewhere and withstand the main threat. Moreover,
the British were conscious that their financial position was not what it
had been before the First World War, when the country had possessed
enormously valuable, and in the last resort encashable, assets all over
the world. If another long war came, Britain must be able to earn her
living. Nothing in the demeanour of the United States Government,
public or private, encouraged any belief that America would intervene
decisively in another war, or sustain its financial burden, without which
the Allies could hardly have fought out the years 1917 and 1918.
Indeed, the neutrality legislation encouraged precisely the opposite
belief. No British government of the 1930s could sensibly count on any
other assumption.

Before the end of 1934, therefore, the main enemy had for better or
worse been identified and, as events proved, rightly identified; the
attempt to reach a closer accommodation with Japan had almost certainly failed, and it seemed likely that no further naval agreements
would be possible; and the CID had instructed its sub-committees to
complete by 1939 preparations for a possible war with Germany.
Though the magnitude of the problem, and not least of the financial
problem, was not at all realised, this was the essential basis upon which
British defence planning went forward. If the time had been wrongly
judged, or the enemy wrongly identified, the results might well have
been fatal. The argument that finance and economic staying power
constituted the fourth arm of defence, a view widely accepted among
ministers and apparently confirmed by the experiences of the Great
War, was bound to place in the hands of the Treasury a strong lever, and
the position of the Chancellor as an able, resourceful and industrious
minister who knew his own mind and was not afraid to face the consequences of decision, 'the pack horse in our great affairs' as Mr Churchill
called him, accentuated that primacy.

Understandably, most ministers and Chiefs of Staff would disclaim
any competence to assess the financial consequences of this or that
policy. Ministers in the spending departments, as usual, were only too
pleased at the prospect of having more money to spend. The War Office,

the Admiralty and the Air Ministry remained, however, notoriously reluctant to present any agreed list of priorities and still less could they arrive at an accepted strategic doctrine; the impression is left that however much departments might grumble at the restraints imposed by the Treasury, they were glad to have somebody to lay down at least the rudiments of a doctrine and an order of priorities, since there could clearly be no coherent programme of rearmament without both.

Events in 1935 demonstrated how precarious and humiliating Britain's position had become. Her very weakness encouraged potential enemies in policies which they would scarcely have dared to attempt earlier. It is hard to believe that Mussolini would have seized Abyssinia in defiance of Britain and France in, say, 1927 or 1932; but in those days neither Britain nor France had reason to pay a high price for Italy's goodwill, whereas the French — notwithstanding all the fine language about collective security — understood perfectly that they would get little or nothing by way of additional security from Britain, and that they could not afford to estrange Italy when a greater threat lay across the Rhine. Mussolini was exploiting the increased bargaining power, the greater freedom of manoeuvre, conferred upon him by the rise of Hitler and the general fear of Germany. The Führer claimed mendaciously in conversation with Sir John Simon and Mr Eden during March 1935 that Germany had already attained parity in the air with Britain. Intelligence available to the Foreign Office differed widely from the reports reaching the Air Ministry and seemed to show that Germany had the capacity to increase output rapidly. Sir John Simon wrote solemnly to the Prime Minister:

> One may have considerable doubts whether once left behind by Germany in the air we shall ever be able to attain a level of parity with her again.
> The conclusion which might have to be drawn . . . is that this country is seriously open to the threat of sudden attack by a Continental Power, in a degree to which it has not been exposed for hundreds of years.[6]

The Naval Agreement with Germany had from a British point of view the advantage of giving a margin for the fulfilment of commitments in the Far East, always assuming that Germay kept to the terms. The same reasoning about the need to preserve a fleet which could meet Japan on level terms caused the Admiralty to advise Mr Baldwin, Prime Minister from June 1935, that in a contest with Italy the British fleet might lose several capital ships, which could not be replaced inside four or five years. This argument probably did more than any other to persuade Baldwin that the risk of a war with Italy could not be run. He had long since recorded his unease, in public and in private, about the danger of being asked to apply sanctions without knowing what the United States was going to do. He understood that the application of telling economic sanctions is inseparable from a willingness to threaten force or to use it. In short, military advice and the foreign policy actually pursued might easily conflict; for the logic of a faithful fulfil-ment of the Covenant would have meant a willingness to face war with Italy, whereas the logic of the government's strategic advice would have been to keep Italian goodwill at almost any price. Small wonder, then, that the policy actually pursued in 1935 and 1936 hesitated between timidity and firmness, failing in the end either to defend Abyssinia or to purchase the goodwill, or even the neutrality, of Italy.

It is in this fashion that the simmering threats in the Far East, the crisis in the Mediterranean, and the fear of Germany are linked; in their different ways, the hollowness of the Stresa Agreement, the muted re-action to Germany's rearmament, the decision to seek agreement with Hitler about the size of the German Navy, the reluctance to confront Italy, the inability to exert a greater leverage on France, and eventually the failure to contest Germany's reoccupation of the Rhineland Zone, the last physical security enjoyed by the victors of 1919, all these acts of policy reacted upon each other. The Royal Air Force was equipped with obsolescent wooden biplanes; the Army had practically no troops fit for despatch to Europe; and in one of those naval metaphors which Admiral Chatfield used to employ, the Navy was stretched bar taut. A policy of greater daring might well have been the right one; Italy had placed a great army on the far side of the Suez Canal. If she had been openly opposed, to the point of war if necessary, the effect upon others might well have been salutary. Nevertheless, it is very hard to blame the ministers of the time for the decisions which they took in the late summer of 1935, though easy and more just to blame them for their failure to apprehend in time the scale and scope of the rearmament which Britain needed to undertake. There was simply not enough margin of strength to allow a calculated risk; the alternative policy would have been a gamble, and, like other gambles, might have paid very handsomely or might have failed very badly.

To those who could not see how Britain was to prepare simultan-eously for the defence of her interests in the east and the defence of her home territories and of western Europe, the possible addition of Italy to the list of enemies converted an unmanageable situation into a nightmare. Thus it became the task of foreign policy to buy time, and to minimise the number of potential enemies. The fact that these attempts were made from a position of known feebleness rendered their success improbable. As the Permanent Under-Secretary at the Foreign Office wrote in August, 1935:

> This country has been so weakened of recent years that we are in no position to take a strong line in the Mediterranean . . . We should be very cautious as to how far and in what manner we force the pace in Paris, with an unreliable France and an unready England.[7]

The British government had thus far announced only modest increases in the strength of the services. Baldwin spent the summer brooding simultaneously about the threat of war with Italy and the timing of the general election, which took place soon after Italy had invaded Abyssinia. Although the Prime Minister decided against making rearmament the principal plank of the government's platform, as Neville Chamberlain had urged, he did make it plain that substantial increases in defence spending were indispensable. The government was returned with its majority reduced, as was inevitable, but still amply sufficient for all purposes.

The dangerous gaps between promise and performance nevertheless remained; the Defence Requirements Committee was undertaking another and still more sombre review of the prospects; and towards the end of November, when tension between Britain and Italy was acute, the Committee reported that Germany's vastly increased strength might portend 'a possibility of attack so continuous and concentrated and on such a scale that a few weeks of such an experience might so undermine the popular morale of our civilian population as to make it difficult for the government to continue the war'. Large further increases in the first line air strength and in naval building were recommended. 'It is a cardinal requirement of our national and Imperial security', said the Committee, 'that our foreign policy should be so conducted as to avoid the possible development of the situation in which we might be confronted simultaneously with the hostility of Japan in the Far East, Germany in the west and any power on the main line of communication between the two.' This amounted to saying that Italy must be bought off; it was a policy perhaps somewhat inglorious but also prudent.[8]

Within little more than a fortnight there followed the Hoare-Laval pact, the moving spirit behind which was Sir Robert Vansittart. His constant refrain, and one to which events lent much point, was that Britain could not afford the luxury of another enemy. This was to talk a language which the British understood less well than the French. It had little to do with morality or with the Covenant, with the defence of the weak against aggression, with the collective enforcement of international law. That was not only the diet upon which ministers of all parties had fed the British public for many years; it was also a cause which appealed to generous instincts, and one which might readily be supported by tough-minded people who wanted to teach Mussolini a lesson in order to deter Hitler.

At all events, the attempt to buy off Italy proved to be a disaster. The Cabinet, having first determined to support Hoare, faced a considerable parliamentary revolt. The Foreign Secretary was compelled to resign, the state of tension with Italy persisted and within three months Germany had moved troops into the Rhineland zone. While the Royal Navy was at war stations in the Mediterranean, the British could neither deploy any effective strength in the Far East, nor adequately protect home waters. Baldwin is reported to have said to the French Foreign Minister that even if there was a one in a hundred chance of war, he dare not take the risk.

There is however this difference between the British response to the crisis in the Rhineland, and the British response to the attack on Abyssinia. It is not likely that in the former case Britain would have been willing to support France with military force even had she possessed the means; whereas if Britain had enjoyed an ample margin of naval strength, or if there had been no difficulties in the Far East, it is probable that Mussolini would have been prevented from taking Abyssinia; but then it is improbable that he would have made the attempt in so blatant a form.

In may seem astonishing in these circumstances that the Defence Requirements Committee did not in its report of November 1935 urge the immediate addition of Italy to the list of probable enemies. There was an element of unreality, perhaps of necessary unreality, in the report. The most likely naval dangers, so it was argued, came from Germany and Japan; and although Hankey, Fisher, Vansittart and the Chiefs of Staff were agreed that Italy was no longer a friendly power, they did not recommend that she should be regarded as an enemy for reasons which, bared to the bone, amounted to saying that there would be no point in so regarding Italy because Britain could not in the fore-

seeable future take adequate precautions against Germany and Japan
and Italy. In other words, Britain's potential liabilities were so great
that she had no means of insuring against them. The Chiefs of Staff
advised during the Rhineland crisis that if there was 'the smallest
danger' of being drawn into a war with Germany, Britain must at once
disengage from her present responsibilities in the Mediterranean which
had 'exhausted practically the whole of our meagre forces'.[9] It need
hardly be added that nothing could suit Hitler better than to see the
two guarantor powers of Locarno at each other's throat.

By this stage the Cabinet had determined upon yet another rearmament programme, which would cost the better part of £1,000 million,
at the values of 1936, over five years. So much for all the careful
hagglings over a million pounds here and two million pounds there of
less than two years before! There was still no sign that the services could
agree on a programme or a doctrine. As the Chancellor of the Exchequer
used to remark, with a justified sense of grievance, the chiefs of staff
tended to submit aggregate plans rather than joint plans.

By the spring of 1936, just before the Germans moved into the
Rhineland zone, the pressure for some better control of defence
spending had become irresistible. Hence the appointment of Sir
Thomas Inskip, after some little delay, to the office of Minister for the
Co-ordination of Defence. Churchill, who had hoped to hold the post
himself and doubtless to convert it into something more substantial, was
alleged to have remarked, 'Mr Baldwin is engaged in searching for a man
of abilities inferior to his own. This herculean task is of necessity
occupying some time.'

The comment, like most of those made since, was grossly unfair to
Inskip. Neither he nor anyone else could tell with certainty whether the
deep apprehensions entertained about the effects of bombardment from
the air would prove justified in practice. If ministers took literally all
that was recommended to them by the best expert opinion, they would
have had to expect from concentrated air bombardment something like
the effects which we should now anticipate from limited nuclear warfare. The fact that the British were willing in certain circumstances to go
to war in 1938, and certainly willing to go to war if all else failed in
1939, indicates that by then fear of bombing was not the determinant
of policy; but that was after radar had been proved effective.

For a period of two years after German reoccupation of the Rhineland Britain's overseas interests were threatened by no crisis of the first
order save, perhaps, the Spanish Civil War; and the policy pursued in
that connection was one of deep caution, based partly upon the fear of

a general war for which Britain was hopelessly unprepared, partly upon
the conviction that whatever arms she could manufacture must be
reserved for her own defence, and partly upon a conviction that even if
General Franco eventually won with the aid of German and Italian
troops and arms, Spain would not become a puppet. Eden was fond of
quoting the Duke of Wellington's remark that there is no country in
which foreigners may interfere with so little profit.

The summer of 1937, however, may be said to inaugurate the last
phase of British policy before the war. The Imperial Conference
indicated no willingness on the part of the dominions to underwrite
British commitments in Europe; Japan resumed open warfare in China;
assurances were somewhat rashly given to Australia and New Zealand
that in time of crisis, no matter what the consequences in the Mediterranean, a strong British fleet would be despatched to the Far East; and
the hope of reaching easier relations with Germany through the planned
visit to London of Foreign Minister Neurath failed.

Moreover, the expenditure on defence, now estimated to cost
£1,500,000 over the five-year period, threatened to escape all control.
There were serious differences of view between the services; the esti-
mates were soaring up almost every day; and there was still no satisfactory agreement about strategic priorities. Senior officials of the
Treasury expressed grave doubts about Britain's capacity to finance the
defence programme and were not alone in wondering what the British
were going to do if they completed it by 1940 and then had to maintain the forces and equipment at that level.

These were the circumstances in which Chamberlain succeeded
Baldwin as prime minister. He believed that the times were too far gone
and too dangerous for a continuation of his predecessor's more easy-
going methods. Indeed, Baldwin in his last year of office had been
mentally and physically unequal to the strains. In the summer of 1936
he had suffered a complete nervous breakdown and had done no work
for three months. From the beginning of 1937 he was counting the
hours to the day of release like an unhappy boy at a boarding school. It
is no doubt true that Chamberlain's methods helped to crystallise and
focus the fluid forces within the government. He gave new point, and a
much more vigorous public expression, to the policy of appeasement.
What he did not do was to invent it. Moreover, and contrary to the
general supposition, he listened carefully to, and assimilated the sense of,
the gloomy military advice which the Chiefs of Staff and Hankey
pressed upon him. It is even arguable that he should have taken this
advice rather less to heart, as Churchill would probably have done.

Whatever its deficiencies, appeasement in the circumstances of 1937, 1938 and 1939 was a policy heartily approved, and frequently recommended, by the service departments. It is certain that Chamberlain, like most men of his generation, felt an abhorrence of modern war and a deep reluctance to embark upon it unless every conceivable alternative had been exhausted. It is probably true that he conceived himself to have some mission to prevent that disaster. There is however no evidence that he regarded appeasement, in the sense of satisfying other powers' grievances at the expense of third parties, as a policy to be pursued everywhere regardless of circumstances, or as dictated by the higher morality. Hence the revealing remark, 'If only we could get on terms with the Germans, I would not care a rap for Musso.'[10]

When the Foreign Secretary urged that preparations must be made for war against Italy, fearing that if Britain and France became embroiled with Mussolini, Hitler might take the opportunity 'to embark on adventures likely to precipitate a general conflict', Chamberlain remarked that the ideal course would be preparation to fight Germany or Italy or Japan, separately or together. That however was a counsel of perfection impossible to follow because Britain had neither the physical nor the financial resources. Since he continued to regard Germany as the greatest potential danger, it followed that Britain's first priority must be preparation against that country.

Chamberlain recognised from the outset that it might well not be possible to get on to better terms with Germany; in which event he had some hopes of detaching Italy from Germany. Hankey argued vigorously for a policy which would allow Britain at least another two years (i.e. to the late summer of 1939), the minimum period which must elapse before she would feel more safe. No more than the Chiefs of Staff did he doubt that Britain could defeat Italy if the two powers were left alone in the ring; but since to secure victory would mean the uncovering of more vital interests elsewhere, world war would almost certainly be precipitated and for that Britain was wholly unprepared.

The approaches to Mussolini which Chamberlain initiated in late July 1937, by means of the letter to Mussolini, represented something of a change of front on the Prime Minister's part and arose from the fear that mutual antagonisms and suspicions might precipitate a war in the Mediterranean almost immediately. Chamberlain's manuscript notes place it beyond doubt that he had been directly influenced by the alarm of the Chiefs of Staff, who had been 'most emphatic that better relations essential especially during the period of rearmament'. Of course, the effort might come to nothing:

But in view of the enormous interests involved, including the safety of this country and its communications with the Far East, and the frightful cost of rearmament, the burden of which has not by any means been fully felt as yet, we should be gravely wanting in our duty if we failed to make every effort to reach a favourable understanding.[11]

Submarine piracy in the Mediterranean a few weeks later allowed the British and French, for once, to exploit the one arm in which they were manifestly stronger than Germany and Italy combined; the projected conversations with Italy were necessarily held up; and Chamberlain, who had less hope of useful American intervention than Eden, drew only limited comfort from President Roosevelt's speech at Chicago, during which he referred to the possibility of putting aggressors in quarantine. The Prime Minister commented, in a masterly example of English understatement:

seeing that patients suffering from epidemic diseases do not normally go about fully armed, is there not a difference here and something lacking in his analogy? . . . Now in the present state of European affairs with the two dictators in a thoroughly nasty temper we simply cannot afford to quarrel with Japan and I very much fear therefore that after a lot of bally-hoo the Americans will somehow fade out and leave us to carry all the blame and the odium . . . [12]

Even the sinking of an American gunboat in the Yangtse, an event which at least proved that America too possessed gunboats, did not move President Roosevelt's administration to any vigorous riposte. Chamberlain's oft-quoted remark, 'it is always best and safest to count on *nothing* from the Americans except words', made in the context of the sinking of the *Panay* and in a letter which went on to express the hope that there might be a change of attitude, was not the contemptuous expression of a Prime Minister who did not care whether or not Britain had American help, but the resigned observation of a minister who had long since come to the conclusion that short of a direct attack upon Hawaii or Honolulu, the United States was unlikely to enter into a great war.[13]

Everything which happened between 1937 and 1941 points to the correctness of that conclusion. When President Roosevelt made his celebrated initiative in January 1938, it was neither likely in itself to lead to any improvement in international relations nor intended to be the har-

binger of active involvement in European politics and still less the pre-
lude to armed intervention in the Far East or in Europe. Chamberlain's
reply might certainly have been more tactfully phrased, the whole business better handled. Nevertheless, there is no evidence that Roosevelt
was deeply shocked by the British response or that relations with the
United States were seriously damaged. To write, as Mr Churchill did in
the afterglow of intimate collaboration with the United States during
the war, of Chamberlain's waving away of the proffered hand stretched
out across the Atlantic, is anachronistic. Whether a different kind of
response might in the end have produced a proffered hand is of course
a matter for argument; the overwhelming *likelihood* is that it would
not.

Meanwhile, Sir Thomas Inskip had been investigating the rearmament programmes on behalf of the cabinet. The object of sound
strategy is to enable a nation to use sufficient force in the right place at
the opportune time. A comforting aggregate of force is of no use if
dispersed so widely that it cannot be concentrated; the ability to fight a
long war is of no comfort to a power unable to withstand a knock-out
blow in the first round. When Eden spoke earnestly to him about the
darkening international outlook in November 1937, Chamberlain
referred to the financial position. To this Eden retorted, most charac-
teristically, that a good financial position would be of small consola-
tion if London were laid flat because the RAF had not been strong
enough. When the Chiefs of Staff argued once again that there was no
prospect of raising forces strong enough to safeguard Britain's territory,
trade and vital interests against Germany, Italy and Japan, Eden replied
that a surrender to one of these powers might be the signal for con-
certed action on the part of all three to secure further sacrifices. He
admitted that Britain might have to acquiesce in more than one fait
accompli, which must presumably have meant that a degree of German
expansion, or an extension of Japanese control in China, would have to
be accepted. It would be better to tolerate for the time being the state
of armed truce and:

> to trust that our own armed strength and that of our associates on
> the one side, and the natural hesitations and potential divergences of
> interest on the part of the other three aggressive Powers on the other
> . . . will maintain some kind of equilibrium and make it possible for
> international differences, as they arise, to be settled without a
> war.[14]

Here lay part of the disagreement between Eden and the Prime Minister, who doubted whether the equilibrium could be maintained in this way and had almost instinctive suspicions of French strength, enhanced by France's inability to manage her currency or to keep a government. He judged Britain to be facing a rising market and there is no evidence in the German or Italian papers so far published to indicate that either Hitler or Mussolini would be content to settle international differences as they arose, or to allow the British so to manage affairs that the equilibrium of Europe would be more or less maintained while British armed strength was built up. On the contrary, and if we take the minutes of the Hossbach meeting as a rough guide, Hitler had every intention of extracting concessions, by war or the credible threat of war, while he had a lead in armaments. He referred hopefully to the prospect of a Mediterranean war as one of those contingencies which would allow Germany to expand in central Europe sooner than would otherwise be possible.

His analysis of British weaknesses was shrewd. He did not share the view, he said, that the British Empire was unshakeable. The mother land was able to protect her colonial possessions not by her own power but only in alliance with the United States. 'How, for instance, could Britain alone defend Canada against attack by America, or her far eastern interests if attacked by Japan?' As significant indications that the Empire could not maintain its position by power politics, he cited the struggle of Ireland for independence, the constitutional tussles in India, the weakening by Japan of Britain's position in the Far East, and the rivalry in the Mediterranean with Italy who was expanding her position of power and thus inevitably coming increasingly into conflict with British interests.[15] Had the language been adjusted somewhat, the document might also have been written in the offices of the Committee of Imperial Defence.

Between December 1937 and February 1938, largely for financial reasons, the Cabinet once again refashioned its list of strategic priorities. Defence of the territories of Britain's allies took a fourth place after defence of the British Isles, the main trade routes, and British and Commonwealth overseas territories. There was scarcely any serious provision for an expeditionary force to be available for warfare in Europe. This state of affairs was accepted, no doubt with deep reluctance, by the whole cabinet. Even Eden, whose anxiety to sustain France was not in doubt, was driven to admit that the position was quite different from that before 1914. Sir Thomas Inskip remarked that if despite these decisions an army eventually had to go to France, the government of the day would certainly be criticised for having neglected to provide against so obvious a contingency.[16] The Foreign Secretary, therefore, did not stand out for the equipment at whatever cost of a large continental army; he did battle hard for staff talks, in the process accusing the Chiefs of Staff — who advised that such talks would merely alienate Germany without producing a useful result — of wishing to recast British foreign policy 'and to clamber on the bandwagon with the Dictators, even though that process meant parting company with France and estranging our relations with the United States'.[17]

In this context it becomes easier to understand the departure of the Foreign Secretary from the government in February. He would have resigned, but for the need to keep the exchanges secret, after the petering out of President Roosevelt's initiative in January; and although he would not have disagreed with Chamberlain's assessment of the very high stakes for which Britain was playing in trying to establish better relations with Italy, he could not credit that any useful object would be achieved by the methods which the rest of the Cabinet favoured. The Far Eastern situation weighed heavily on the Prime Minister who, when pressing once more for an early beginning to the talks with Mussolini, noted, 'it will be as well, for the Japs are growing more and more insolent and brutal'. In early January, Chamberlain ruled that a fleet should not be sent to Singapore because that would deprive Britain of her strongest card in bargaining with Italy. At the long Cabinet meeting which preceded Eden's resignation, Chamberlain said that he was influenced by the general state of military unpreparedness and the growing financial burden of the armament programme, which bade fair to undermine Britain's greatest asset, strong credit. Eden's counter-argument had much force; its weakness lay in the simple fact that the more precautions Britain took against Italy in the Mediterranean and Middle East, the less able she would be to defend her interests against Germany or Japan. His departure from office was followed by the negotiation of an agreement with Italy, of limited scope and value.

Meanwhile, Hitler, whom Italy's deep embroilment in Spain suited down to the ground, had seized Austria. Cadogan, now Permanent Under-Secretary of the Foreign Office, came to the conclusion, after days and nights of agonising, that Britain should not offer a guarantee to Czechoslovakia. 'We *must* not precipitate a conflict now — we shall be smashed.'[18] The Chiefs of Staff, more elaborately, reported in much the same sense. The Cabinet accepted that advice. Nothing that France or Britain could do, Chamberlain wrote, could save Czechoslovakia from being overrun by a determined Germany. To give a guarantee would therefore 'simply be a pretext for going to war with Germany. That we could not think of unless we had a reasonable prospect of being able to beat her to her knees in a reasonable time, and of that I see no sign'.

If we took this letter as our sole guide to the Cabinet's motives, we should have to conclude that strategic advice was the dominant fact. However, this account must be balanced against the long disquisition which Chamberlain delivered to French ministers at the end of April 1938. Though much of the reasoning was similar, it did not lay the weight so exclusively on military considerations.[19]

For the next six months the position of the Cabinet remained the same. Britain would neither promise belligerency if Czechoslovakia were invaded nor promise neutrality. Fortified by his study of Professor Temperley's new biography of Canning, Chamberlain judged the situation too dangerous for bluff. 'I am satisfied that we should be wrong to allow the most vital decision that any country could take, the decision as to peace or war, to pass out of our own hands into those of the ruler of another country and a lunatic at that.'[20]

The advice of the military staffs remained constant; that Britain should if humanly possible avoid a major war in 1938. It is arguable, though the German documents hardly support the conclusion, that if the Cabinet had determined to override their advice, Hitler's policy would have been shown up as a bluff, or that a coup in Germany would have removed him. At all events the decision not to fight over the Czechoslovak issue in the autumn was approved by the British ambassadors in every major country of Europe, and in Tokyo and Washington; by the Permanent Under-Secretary of the Foreign Office and the Foreign Secretary; and by each of the Chiefs of Staff. Not until a very late stage, just before the Munich meeting, did Chamberlain tell Hitler through Sir Horace Wilson that if Czechoslovakia were invaded, France would honour her obligation and Britain would fight at once. Hitler's angry retort shows plainly that he understood.[21] The threat was issued only after the cession of the Sudetenland to Germany had been agreed.

It does not necessarily follow from all this that if Britain had been strong enough to enjoy a reasonable prospect of beating Germany to her knees in a reasonable time, Chamberlain and his colleagues would have gone to war over the Czechoslovak issue. Even in those circumstances they might have judged that so terrible an event must be avoided until it was established beyond all doubt that Germany intended to dominate Europe by force. On the other hand, it is clear that the buying of time was a substantial ingredient of British policy;

that is what Chamberlain meant by remarking to the French Prime Minister in April that he thought a time would come 'when a gamble on the issue of peace and war might be contemplated with less anxiety than at present'.

The winter after Munich was marked by a further acceleration of rearmament. The Prime Minister, sanguine by temperament, hoped in his more optimistic moods for a period of peace, or at any rate did not regard war as inevitable, while the Cabinet in those few months took a whole series of decisions which would have seemed inconceivable even a short while before. The Chancellor of the Exchequer warned the Cabinet in November that the reserves had been heavily depleted by the withdrawal of foreign capital from Britain. Despite enormous expenditure on rearmament, the general level of her economic activity was in fact lower than it had been in 1937. Nevertheless, it is not hard to detect an improvement in confidence in the reports rendered by the Chiefs of Staff. They were by no means keen to go to war in 1939; most of the military and diplomatic advisers of the government would have preferred to postpone the issue for another year or two if they could; but the Chiefs of Staff did advise that Britain should go to war if Germany invaded Holland, even if such intervention brought in Italy and perhaps Japan as well.

There is a sense in which, from 1935 to 1936, French policy towards Germany had rested in British hands, because no French government was likely to face war with the German army unless assured of British support. By the same token, however, Britain depended on the French army and because of that very fact had to abandon the policy of building up a first-class air force and a first-class navy, but without a continental army. In the celebrated phrase, 'un effort du sang' was needed. Otherwise, French morale might sag and the protection of the French army be lost. The decision to equip a British expeditionary force was finally taken in February 1939, well before the seizure of Prague. The financial argument had in the end been displaced.

It is normal to refer to the programme for the spending of £1,500 million over five years on which the Cabinet had agreed in 1937, or to the increased estimate of £1,650 million accepted at the beginning of 1938; what is less often noticed is that, at the rate of expenditure authorised for 1939, the aggregate for the five years would have been nearer to £3,000 million. Ironically enough, the point at which financial limits were for all practical purposes abandoned was just the time at which there was the gravest reason to fear for the economy. How such expenditure was to be sustained, and especially if Britain should be shortly involved in a long war, no one could explain. Had the United States not come to the rescue in the latter part of 1940, the British Empire could not have maintained its war effort. Broadly speaking, and with all the benefit of hindsight, it is impossible to say that the limits set by the Treasury upon rearmament were unreasonable or unnecessary.

After the seizure of Prague, there occurred another symbolic shift of policy. Despite the assurances given in 1937, the governments of Australia and New Zealand had to be told that although it would be the intention of Britain to uphold them and to defend her interests in the Far East, the composition, strength and time of despatch of the fleet to the Far East would have to depend on the circumstances prevailing at the time. As for the guarantees given successively to Poland, Rumania, Greece and Turkey, they did in one sense constitute (to use Chamberlain's phrase) a revolution in British foreign policy. After all, this was the first occasion on which the British had undertaken to guarantee frontiers in eastern and south-eastern Europe. But nobody, least of all the Poles, supposed that the British could deploy a substantial army in the plains of Poland, the mountains of Greece, or even across the Rhine. The guarantees were surely intended as warnings to Hitler and, after the seizure of Albania, to Mussolini, that further assaults would be the signal for general war. The guarantee to Poland, offered in the mistaken belief that a German attack on that country might be imminent, did not derive from any compelling military reason, though equally it was not given against military advice.

It would be a tempting excursus, but beyond the scope of this chapter, to dwell on the inadequacies of Britain's methods of collecting and interpreting military and political intelligence in those days. Polish military strength was somewhat overestimated, and that of Russia underestimated. The Chiefs of Staff, though their view of the value of an alliance with Russia did change, had never urged that any high price should be paid for it. There is neither evidence nor probability that if Britain had failed to guarantee Poland, she and France would have been able to make satisfactory terms in Moscow during the summer of 1939. Russia too had to consider whether the border clashes with Japan would erupt into something more serious. As for the British government, they certainly wished to prevent Russia from coming to terms with Germany, and in the later stages they lacked hard and timely intelligence – which the Americans possessed – of the conversations between the German and Russian governments. Nothing in the military advice would have led ministers to imagine that Russia was capable of mounting a successful offensive outside her own borders, though it was generally accepted, and had been for some time, that the Red Army would fight doughtily in defence of Russian soil.

Despite the belated decision to introduce conscription, the essential British weakness in the talks, befogged as they were by twenty years of well-founded suspicion and marked on the British side by grudging concession of points which would have been better given up earlier, lay in the inability to place a large army on the continent of Europe. Even so, it is possible that the negotiations might have ended in success if Hitler had refused to join in the bargaining. Once he had decided to offer terms, nothing that anyone else could produce would be likely to match their attraction for Stalin. There is no sign that the British government was intending to divert Germany to a career of conquest in the East, as Stalin successfully diverted Germany for a time to a career of conquest in the West. Indeed, on the advice which the British government received it would have been foolish to do so, since neither Poland nor Russia was thought capable of sustained resistance to Germany.

As for the Far East, the British continued to play for time. There was one point during that summer when the situation at Tientsin became so threatening that the despatch of a fleet was considered. In the end, however, with the general fear that the hour of danger in Europe would come at the end of August, and the negotiations in Moscow dragging on interminably, the Cabinet decided that nothing but the most determined assault by Japan on British interests would justify the sending of capital ships to the other end of the world. As Chamberlain recorded, 'It is maddening to have to hold our hands in the face of such humiliations but we cannot ignore the terrible risks of putting such temptations in Hitler's way.'[22] He continued to hope that the combination of the guarantees and British rearmament would exercise its deterrent effect upon Germany, and to be thankful that Britain had not been compelled to fight a year earlier:

> The longer the war is put off the less likely it is to come at all as we go on perfecting our defences, and building up the defences of our Allies . . . You don't need offensive forces sufficient to win a smashing victory. What you want are defensive forces sufficiently strong to make it impossible for the other side to win except at such a cost as to make it not worth while.[23]

When it became known that Germany and Russia were about to sign a pact, Chamberlain felt the burden of 1914 and wished to ensure that whatever might befall there should be no ground for the charge that if only Britain had made her position clear in advance the catastrophe might have been avoided. He had indeed been discussing this aspect in his family circle for the preceding nine or twelve months.[24] He wrote at once to Hitler:

> His Majesty's Government are resolved that on this occasion there shall be no such tragic misunderstanding. If the case should arise, they are resolved and prepared to employ without delay all the forces at their command, and it is impossible to foresee the end of hostilities once they are engaged.[25]

The fact that Germany did, for the moment, pay a high price at Moscow indicates either that Hitler believed the British and French would take their obligation to Poland seriously, or that he simply wished to free himself in the East so as to snuff out those whom he had described in 1937 as his hate-inspired antagonists. It is easy to deduce from all the disasters and defeats of 1940 that the military position of September 1939 was a hopeless one. In fact, it might have been worse from the British point of view. Certainly Hitler had made the British and French delegations in Moscow look ridiculous by signing his pact with Stalin, so that they had to slink off while Ribbentrop and Stalin congratulated each other. Germany was joined, however, neither by Japan nor by Italy. The conjunction which the Chiefs of Staff and their ministerial masters had so long feared did not come to pass in the early part of the war. Germany had not informed her anti-comintern partners that she was about to sup with the devil; the Japanese government fell and Mussolini, conscious of being treated with contempt, authorised his son-in-law and foreign minister, Count Ciano, to tell the British that Italy was going to remain neutral.

The Nazi-Soviet pact certainly did nothing to reduce determination and morale in Britain, except among the Communists, who were anyway very few in number and who, given the extreme secrecy with which the business had been conducted, were not able to receive instructions in time from Moscow and therefore ran about like decapitated chickens for several days before the officially approved line arrived. In all the countries where Roman Catholic influence was powerful, and not least in Spain and Italy, the shock reverberated. Had Franco joined in the war openly on the German side, and allowed German troops to cross Spain, Gibraltar must have fallen and with it the British capacity to sustain the war in the Mediterranean.

It may well be asked why it was if the position in the autumn of 1939 was not as unsatisfactory as it might have been from a military point of view, that by the summer of 1940 Britain and the Commonwealth countries were left alone to fight against Hitler and Mussolini? To this entirely pertinent question there are no doubt many answers. Probably it would have been wise for the British and French to declare war on Italy in the winter of 1939-40 and destroy as much as they could of the Italian fleet and air force. That course, however, would have involved the deliberate overriding of the Chiefs of Staff and all the members of the War Cabinet, including Mr Churchill, endorsed the policy of upholding Italy's neutrality. One crucial fact upset the whole basis on which British strategy, and Churchill's strategy at least as much as Chamberlain's, had rested: the collapse of France. When in the spring of 1939 the British planning staffs, assuming Italian belligerency from the outset, had tried to lay down a sound strategy for a long war, they distinguished three phases: the first, in which the allies would hold out and weather the early hammer-blows; a second, during which Italy's African empire would be overrun, and Italy knocked out of the war, the bombing force being used against Germany; and the third, during which Germany would be defeated and everything possible would be done to seek and ensure the help of the United States. With every allowance for all the unforeseen variations, including Hitler's attack on Russia and Japan's upon the United States, that was not bad forecasting.

May I close with a word of caution? This chapter has dealt, often in a cursory way, with some aspects of British diplomacy and strategy in the ten years before the Second World War. To isolate one particular factor in the making of policy may become as misleading as the reading of those volumes of documents so conveniently segregated by subject. It is never possible to say with certainty, when ministers have to weigh so many aspects, that a decision on some vital issue of foreign policy was taken for a simple and identifiable reason. Though the records are copious, historians should beware of telling themselves and others that they now know the whole story. We are often able to establish the main ingredients of a policy pursued over a considerable period, though even then it is necessary to be watchful for assumptions unconsciously made, or so generally shared as to make it necessary to set them down in detail; what we can never establish is the precise proportion and weight accorded to each argument or factor. Even those full minutes of the Cabinet and its committees are only compressed, and sometimes decorous, records of long conversations. They leave an impression of coherence, clear decision and intellectual discipline. One evening during the Great War, after a somewhat rambling ministerial discussion, Lloyd George rose from the Cabinet table and said 'Well, Maurice, you know what we have decided. Will you do the minutes?' When he returned, a good deal later, he found on the blotting pad this rhyme, written out in Hankey's sprawling and childlike hand:

> And now while the Great Ones depart to their dinner,
> The Secretary sits, growing thinner and thinner,
> Racking his brains to record and report
> What he thinks that they think that they ought to have thought.

Bibliographical Note

This paper is based to a large extent upon research undertaken in the last ten years for a book on British foreign policy between the wars and for the forthcoming biography of Neville Chamberlain. I have drawn freely upon the papers of the Cabinet, Cabinet committees, the CID and its sub-committees; the archives of the Foreign Office and to a lesser degree of the Dominions Office, the Treasury and the Service departments. The most useful collections of private papers are those of Sir Austen Chamberlain, Neville Chamberlain (Birmingham University Library), Ramsay MacDonald (Public Record Office), Lord Baldwin (Cambridge University Library), Lord Halifax (private possession, with microfilm copies of some of the documents at the University Libraries of Cambridge and Leeds), Lord Simon (private possession), Lord Templewood (Cambridge University Library), Lord Hankey (Churchill College, Cambridge). There are numerous other useful collections, especially at Churchill College and King's College, London; and at the Public Record Office, the series Premier I-IV and F.O. 800 contain 'Private Office' papers of prime ministers, foreign secretaries and diplomats.

The published sources are now so numerous that it is not possible to mention more than a few. On general questions of foreign policy, W.N. Medlicott, *British Foreign Policy Since Versailles* (1968, revised edition) and F.S. Northedge, *The Troubled Giant* (1966) remain the best guides. The recently published work by Professor N.H. Gibbs, *Grand Strategy*, Vol. I (HMSO, 1976) is the indispensable starting-point for any discussion of the British strategic position between the wars, though there is still plenty of room for legitimate disagreement about his conclusions. Other works of importance in this field are M. Cowling, *The Impact of Hitler* (1975); D.C. Watt, *Personalities and Policies* (1965), and *Too Serious a Business* (1975); Sir Graham Vincent, *Stanley Baldwin and Rearmament* (unpublished TS in the Library of Leeds University); R. Ovendale, *'Appeasement' and the English-Speaking World* (1975); K. Middlemas, *The Diplomacy of Illusion* (1972); D.H. Aldcroft, *The Inter-War Economy: Britain 1919-1939* (1970); I.M. Drummond, *Imperial Economic Policy, 1917-1939* (1974); B.E.V. Sabine, *British Budgets in Peace and War, 1932-1945* (1970); B. Bond (ed.), *Chief of Staff: The Diaries of Lieutenant-General Sir Henry Pownall*, Vol. 1 (1972); M. Howard, *The Continental Commitment* (1972); A. Trotter, *Britain and East Asia 1933-1937* (1975); R.J. Minney, *The Private Papers of Hore-Belisha* (1960); D.N. Dilks (ed.),

The Diaries of Sir Alexander Cadogan, 1938-1945 (1971); Rt. Hon. Earl of Avon, *Facing the Dictators* (1962); L. Pratt, *East of Malta, West of Suez* (1975). This last work succeeds better than any other, to my mind, in demonstrating the inseparability of the risks in different theatres of possible warfare.

Among biographies, the most helpful are those by D. Marquand on MacDonald, S. Roskill on Hankey, Sir K. Feiling on Chamberlain, R.K. Middlemas and A.J.L. Barnes on Baldwin. J.A. Cross on Sir S. Hoare and E.B. Segel on Sir J. Simon both have substantial new material. As for articles in learned journals, it is impossible to pick out more than a few from the several hundreds dealing with aspects of British foreign and defence policy in the 1930s: S. Roskill, 'Imperial Defence 1910-1950' in *The Round Table*, 1970; U. Bialer, 'The Danger of Bombardment from the Air and the Making of British Air Disarmament Policy, 1932-1934' in B. Bond and I. Roy (eds.), *War and Society* (1975); G. Niedhart, 'Der Bundniswert der Sowjetunion in Urteil Grossbritanniends 1936-1939' in *Milikargeschichtliche Mitteilungen*, 1971; A. Marder, 'The Royal Navy and the Ethiopian Crisis of 1936-36' in *The American Historical Review*, 1970; N.H. Gibbs, 'British Strategic Doctrine 1918-1939' in M. Howard (ed.), *The Theory and Practice of War;* anon., 'Appeasement Reconsidered' in *The Round Table*, 1963; F. Coghlan, 'Aramament, Economic Policy and Appeasement: the Background to British Foreign Policy 1931-1937' in *History*, 1972; numerous contributions in *Les Relations Franco-Britanniques de 1935 à 1939* (Paris, 1975); S. Roskill, 'The Ten-Year Rule — the historical facts' in *Journals of the Royal United Services Institute*, 1972. I have also learned much from the dissertations written by undergraduate students in the School of History at Leeds, and from the theses of Dr I. Hamill, Dr J.J. Underwood and Mr P. Bell (all of Leeds), Mr R. Manne and Dr J. Lippincott (Oxford). My kind colleague Dr George Peden has generously allowed me to read his Oxford thesis on the role of the Treasury in the rearmament of the 1930s.

Notes

1. *Documents on British Foreign Policy*, Series II, Vol. IX, pp. 677-8.
2. For Sir John Simon's apprehensions on this score, see C.P. (i.e. Cabinet Paper) 264 (33).
3. On Vansittart, see I. Colvin, *Vansittart in Office* (1965) and W.M. Medlicott, *Britain and Germany, The Search for Agreement* (1969); on Fisher, D.C. Watt, *Personalities and Policies* (1965).
4. Neville Chamberlain's diary, 6 June 1934; I owe this, and other references from his papers, to the courtesy of Birmingham University Library and of Mrs Stephen Lloyd.
5. Neville Chamberlain to Hilda Chamberlain, 12 May 1935.
6. Sir John Simon to Ramsay MacDonald, 10 April 1935; cited in Rt. Hon. Earl of Avon, *Facing The Dictators*, p. 183.
7. Cited in A. Marder, 'The Royal Navy and the Ethiopian Crisis of 1935-36' in *The American Historical Review*, 1970, p. 1329.
8. The DRC's third report was presented on 21 November 1935; for a discussion of the contents, see N.H. Gibbs, *Grand Strategy*, Vol. I, pp. 254 ff.
9. Marden, loc. cit., p. 1352.
10. Sir K. Feiling, *The Life of Neville Chamberlain*, p. 329.
11. Chamberlain's remarks at a meeting of the CID, 5 July 1937, Cab. 2/6; memorandum by Hankey, 19 July 1937, Premier I/276; MS notes by Chamberlain, and amendments to F.O. paper, undated but August 1937,

ibid. I am grateful to Professor L. Pratt for drawing these notes to my attention.

12. Neville Chamberlain to Hilda Chamberlain, 9 October 1937.
13. Neville Chamberlain to Hilda Chamberlain, 17 December 1937; Feiling, op. cit., p. 253.
14. Eden, op. cit., p. 493; memorandum by Eden, 26 November 1937, in F.O. 371/20702.
15. *Documents on German Foreign Policy*, Series D. Vol. I, pp. 32-3.
16. B. Bond, *France and Belgium 1939-1940*, p. 20, draws attention to this pointed and damaging remark.
17. Eden to the Prime Minister, 1 January 1938, Premier I/276.
18. D.N. Dilks (ed.), *The Diaries of Sir Alexander Cadogan*, p. 63.
19. Compare Neville Chamberlain to Ida Chamberlain, 20 March 1938, with *Documents on British Foreign Policy*, Series III, Vol. I, pp. 212 ff.
20. Neville Chamberlain to Ida Chamberlain, 11 September 1938.
21. *Documents on British Foreign Policy*, Series III, Vol. II, p. 550.
22. Neville Chamberlain to Ida Chamberlain, 25 June 1939.
23. Neville Chamberlain to Ida Chamberlain, 23 July 1939.
24. I am obliged for this information to the Vice-Chancellor of Leeds University, Lord Boyle, who learned of it from the late Mrs Neville Chamberlain.
25. *Documents on British Foreign Policy*, Series III, Vol. VII, p. 127.

NOTES ON CONTRIBUTORS

David Dilks has been Professor of International History at the University of Leeds since 1970 and Chairman of the School of History since 1974. He was in the 1960s Research Assistant to Sir Anthony Eden, Marshal of the RAF Lord Tedder, and Mr Harold Macmillan, and taught at the London School of Economics. His published works include a number of articles and reviews; *Curzon in India,* 2 vols. (1969 and 1970); *The Diaries of Sir Alexander Cadogan* (1971); 'Baldwin and Chamberlain' in Lord Butler (ed.), *The Conservatives* (1977). He is writing an authorised biography of Neville Chamberlain and wrote and presented for BBC Television during 1977 eleven programmes about the office of Prime Minister from Lloyd George to the present day. He was Chairman of the Commonwealth Youth Exchange Council from 1968 to 1973 and a Consultant to the Secretary-General of the Commonwealth in 1974 and 1975.

Adrian Preston is Professor of History at the Royal Military College of Canada. In 1971-2, he held the Chair of Military and Strategic Studies at Acadia University, Nova Scotia. His published works include *In Relief of Gordon* (1965); *The South African Diaries of Sir Garnet Wolseley,* 2 vols. (1971 and 1973). He is co-editor (with Peter Dennis) of *Soldiers and Statesmen* (1976), and *Swords and Covenants* (1976) and (with Barry Hunt), *War Aims and Strategy 1914-18* (1977). He is currently editing *The Great War Diaries of Sir Henry Rider Haggard, 1914-18,* and completing a biography of Field Marshal Lord Wolseley.

Albert Seaton is a former professional British Army officer and was a senior associate member of St Antony's College, Oxford, from 1973 to 1977. He is both Russian- and German-speaking and is the author of a number of books on contemporary Russian and German military affairs.

Donald Cameron Watt, M.A., F.R. His. S., Professor of International History in the University of London (L.S.E.), formerly assistant editor, *Documents on German Foreign Policy, 1918-1945;* his books include *Personalities and Policies: Studies in the Formulation of British Foreign Policy in the Twentieth Century,* London, Longmans; South Bend, Indiana, University of Notre Dame Press, 1965; reprint New York

133

Greenwood Press, 1974; *Too Serious a Business, European Armed Force Forces and the Approach of the Second World War,* London, Temple Smith; Berkeley, California, University of California Press, 1975. At present official historian of British defence organisation in the Cabinet Office.

Gerhard L. Weinberg is William Rand Kenan Jr., Professor of History at the University of North Carolina. He has previously taught at the Universities of Michigan, Kentucky and Chicago. His main works include *The Foreign Policy of Hitler's Germany* and *Germany and the Soviet Union, 1939-41.*

John Whittam read history at Worcester College, Oxford, and then spent two years at St Antony's studying for a B.Phil. and writing a dissertation on Farini. After spending a year as an instructor at the University of Pennsylvania, he lectured at London University, first at Royal Holloway and, between 1962 and 1964, at Westfield College. Since 1964, he has been lecturing at Bristol University. In 1967 he completed his Ph.D. (London University), writing a dissertation on Ricasoli. In 1970-1 he was Alistair Horne Fellow at St Antony's engaged in research on the Risorgimento. He has made several visits to Italy, has published articles on Italian history in the period 1861-1945, and his book on *The Politics of the Italian Army* (London, 1977) appeared recently. His teaching commitments include European history since 1815 and a more intensive course on the Fall of France. He is at present engaged on research into Tuscan Fascism and the Anglo-Italian war between 1940 and 1943.

Robert J. Young was educated at the University of Saskatchewan and the London School of Economics. He is currently Associate Professor of History at the University of Winnipeg. His book *In Command of France: French Foreign Policy and Military Planning in the Nazi Years, 1933-1940* is to be published by Harvard University Press in 1978.

INDEX